Be Ready to Parent Twins

Be Ready to Parent Twins

Dr Ella Rachamim and Louise Brown

unbound

This edition first published in 2020

Unbound

TC Group, Level 1, Devonshire House, One Mayfair Place,
London, W1J 8AJ

www.unbound.com

ISBN (eBook): 978-1-78965-082-2

ISBN (Paperback): 978-1-78965-081-5

Cover design by Mecob

Printed and bound in Great Britain by Clays Ltd, Elcograf S.p.A.

Dedicated with all our love to our mums, who parented us through their own challenging times.

Super Patrons

Mcclintock
Gaye McKeogh
midwifebeth.com
Stephanie Modell
Becca Moore
Sabrenia Morgan
Jane Neerkin
Sue Nicol
James Nicoll
Laurence Norman
Sarah Norris
Jemma O'Neill
Toby Osbourn
Ricki Outis
Luisa Pettigrew
Kim Plowright
Paula J Prosser
Roberta Rachamim
Shelley Rifkin
Mabel Rodríguez
Fiona Romeo

Katie Ruback
Claudia Rubenstein
Bethan Ryder
Shelley-Anne Salisbury
Lee Selsick
Deepa Shah
Karen Shamash
David Skinner
Jody Smith
Melony Smith
Victoria Smith
Lynsey Smyth
Geoff Sutton
Kelly Sweeney
Jen Topping
Linh Tran
Glenn Walker
David Walmsley
Polly Wann
Layla West
Christina Young

Contents

Contents

Charlotte's Maternity Services
https://www.charlottes-maternity-services.co.uk/
Twin and Triplet Maternity Nurse and Nanny

Caroline Evans
https://www.carolineelizabethevans.com/
Helping your family flourish!

HushaBoo
https://hushaboo.co.uk/
A Hushed night's sleep for both you and your Boo
– Night Nanny & Sleep Consulting Services

Nanny McHaffee Childcare
http://www.nannymchaffee.com
Household staffing and Childcare Agency

Night Owls (UK) Ltd
www.Nightowls.agency
A good night and may your sleep be sweet

Prologue

People say that nothing prepares you for parenthood. Now think of that unpreparedness... and double it. Twin pregnancies are growing in number thanks to women choosing to become mothers later in life, fertility treatment, the use of surrogates and improvements in medical care for premature infants. In the UK alone, the incidence of multiples has risen so dramatically that now one in every thirty-two babies is a twin or a triplet and that number is set to rise.

This is not an exhaustive guide to all aspects of pregnancy, birth and babyhood – there are already lots of publications that do this – but what we felt was lacking was a source of advice relating each aspect to having twins: from feeding to sleeping to getting mobile.

All twin parents know that the best people to speak to are others who have been there themselves. *Be*

Ready to Parent Twins combines the professional and personal experiences of twin mums Louise Brown and Dr Ella Rachamim (also a paediatrician) to give rounded and practical advice, from coping with pregnancy symptoms to childcare options when going back to work. It also draws on the experiences of other twin mums to include first-person perspectives on premature delivery, planned and emergency C-sections, natural births, bottle feeding and breastfeeding, and a variety of other choices and circumstances. However they've done it, they've all been through it and are still standing and smiling (or lying down – give them a break, sleep deprivation is no joke).

And even if this is not a first pregnancy, take a deep breath while Ella and Louise welcome you to a new world of near-compulsory epidurals, tandem feeding and dealing politely with the army of strangers who say 'Double trouble?' every time you leave the house.

The book will take you through each stage of pregnancy and your first year together, from preparation to the early days, to three months, six months, and finally nine months to one year with tips intended for the particular challenge of managing more than one baby. You can dip into the chapter most relevant to you at each stage – essential when you are a very busy twin parent – but it will also give you a helpful overview during the wait for your bundles of joy to arrive.

We hope you have a supportive co-parent who might read this with you, so we've also included a few comments from our partners if you want to share their perspective or simply see things from their point of view. We'd also like to add that most of the early chapters of the book are addressed with a birth mum in mind, but we also hope that any of you using a surrogate or adopting twins will find useful information to help understand the birth mother's experience and prepare well for your first year.

Our main aim is to share honest, helpful, no-holds-barred advice from those who have been there, to reflect the diversity of parenting experiences and reassure parents that there is more than one way to get it right. We hope our book will support your ability to make the right choices for you and your babies for a happy start to an incredible journey.

Chapter 1: Pregnancy

So, you've found out you're having twins – congratulations and welcome to the multiple parent community; it's a warm and supportive group without competition and full of kindness, acceptance and survival tips.

For some the prospect of more than one baby arriving won't be a shock; for others it will be a jaw-dropping surprise. There may be feelings of excitement and joy alongside fear and anxiety. Commonly there is a period of disbelief and panic, with overwhelming worries of how you will cope practically and financially, plus anxiety over your babies' health and your own.

You may have had a long and emotional journey to become pregnant and so you may be filled with joy but, even then, you may be cautious about becoming *too* happy, alongside the worry about what this means for your life and relationships. If you already have children you may be feeling anxious and guilty about the impact twins may have on them and worrying about the time you will – or rather won't – have for everyone and everything.

This is all normal. It can be a difficult road but the joy of twins *is* more than double, even if it sometimes feels like more than double the work.

***

Ella

At first my biggest worries were the impact on my older son who was under one at the time and how I would ever get out with all three of them. And, especially sharing a placenta, the babies' health and risk of them coming early. I do feel very lucky that my son adores his twin sisters, that they are healthy and that I manage to get out with all three myself, most days, in a reasonable state.

Hugh (Ella's husband)

Obviously the first emotion was surprise and, to tell the truth, I was absolutely delighted. I had always wanted twins. But very quickly I started to think about the practicalities. Would we need to buy a bigger car? Or a bigger house? As we already had one child, I started to wonder how two parents were going to look after three small children. Would we always need a third adult to go with us when we went out with all three kids? I also started to worry about the effect on our young son. I worried he would feel sidelined and neglected as we would have to spend so much time looking after the twins. And I knew that twins attract plenty of attention from other people. Would our little guy feel completely forgotten when everyone paid attention to the twins? But my greatest worry was all the additional risks of a twin pregnancy. I just desperately wanted everything to be alright. Despite all these worries I was really excited. I knew I was about to embark on a wonderful adventure.

Louise

'There's one heartbeat… and there's another heartbeat.' Robert and I were totally shocked to discover we were having twins. After a few failed attempts at IVF after our son, Thomas (also IVF), we were fully expecting this try, our last try, to be unsuccessful – and how wrong we were. We were overwhelmed, overjoyed, panicked about the size of our house but amazed and astounded that we were soon going to be a family of five when we'd spent many years wondering if we would ever have a family at all.

Rob (Louise's husband)
How did I feel? Shocked, disbelieving and pleased.

***

We also asked our panel of mums how they felt when they first found out they were pregnant with twins…

Alison
I was constantly worried one twin wouldn't make it – that was the reason for my anxiety. I think twin pregnancies make you more anxious than singleton ['singleton' meaning one baby – your first bit of twin mum jargon to learn] *ones but I got lots of reassurance and support from the twin midwife at the hospital.*

Jo
I was horrified when I found out. I just couldn't believe it. I sat in the scanning room (I was seven weeks pregnant at the time) and just swore for about fifteen minutes. My husband was at work and I phoned him once the scan was finished. He had a similar reaction and then swore (in his open-plan office) for another fifteen minutes. Basically, it was such a complete shock to us both. We already had a one-year-old son and the addition of twins meant a huge amount of mental adjustment and pushed us into making lots of decisions we hadn't planned on thinking about for a few years. Whilst

we absolutely wouldn't be without them, and realise we are completely blessed to have them, we didn't really intend on having three children. I really like even numbers.

Elna

Absolutely stunned and shocked. I found out at my 12–week scan and I realised because I could see it on the screen before she told us, but my husband couldn't. I saw two sacs so I knew before she said the words and my whole body started shaking and convulsing. I don't think I really came to terms with it until I had them.

Jibecke

It was funny because I tend to do everything over the top, so we said on the way there 'I bet it's going to be twins', and when they said it was I said, 'Of course!'

Lucia

In my case it was a bit of a shock but not so much because I had IVF so I knew it might happen. I don't know why but as soon as I was pregnant I had the feeling it was twins. When I did the test it came up so quickly, I almost didn't touch the stick, so I thought is it not working well? Has it expired or is there something wrong with it? When I went to the scan and I saw the face of the lady, I thought 'yep that's two'. At the beginning you have that sinking feeling, the first thing that comes to mind is what am I going to do with two? Am I going to be able to manage with two babies? I've never even had one!

Vic

We decided to go through a clinic so that our donor (a friend) wouldn't be legally responsible for the children and Ali (my partner) would be legally recognised as a parent. So we knew it was a possibility because we went through the drug regime which gives you a higher chance of having twins, but we had some problems as I'd been pregnant with a singleton and had miscarried when I was five months pregnant.

We had so many scans because of what had happened and I could see it was twins, which was a real mix of elation but also complete nerves! It was amazing there was two of them and we'd been given this second chance but I also knew it would be a really complicated pregnancy and, given what had happened before, there was this chance of losing them which added a layer of complexity.

***

GET READY

Once you tell people you are expecting twins or more

you will be quite the centre of attention. During the final months you will be very tired, very large and may get a little bit tetchy with the repeated comments about your size and the arrival date. Get used to it, the attention only increases once they arrive. People take a lot of interest in twins and can ask quite private questions – one woman at a bus stop asked Louise 'were they natural?' to which she replied with a blow-by-blow account of her vaginal birth only to realise she meant were they conceived by IVF.

But there is something remarkable and exciting about twins and the community seems to feel this. Once they are born, you will be stopped a lot and asked whether they are twins and how you manage, and asked if they are identical or not and so on; be prepared and think about what information you want to share, and how politely to inform them, for example, that, no, boy-girl twins can't be identical.

***

Alison

I love the knowing look of another twin parent out in the park – the look that says, 'I KNOW how hard the work is and how intense it can be, RESPECT to you.' I love it when mums of older twins say, 'Well done! You're doing a great job.'

***

This chapter covers getting ready for your babies' arrival: equipment, twin support groups, reading and resources, the medical process leading up to birth, how to prepare those around you and where to get help. It also covers emotional support around difficult situations including premature delivery and the loss of a twin.

ADVICE AND SUPPORT

The first thing we implore you to do is join your local twins' group – they are an amazing source of support and advice. If you can't find one, ask around, ask midwives or look it up online (TwinsclubUK) or ask Twins Trust (formerly TAMBA, the Twins and Multiple Births Association). Twins clubs are run by parents of twins voluntarily, which means not all areas have them and they vary in activity. There will be a membership fee, but most groups don't expect a payment until the babies are born and it's usually pretty small (and might even be waived in some circumstances, dependent on the group).

You can go along with bump to some coffee mornings or toddler groups, asking questions of those who have done it and are there to tell the tale. These are the best people to talk to about, for example, what a Caesarean or an induction is really like – and may have also delivered in the same hospital you're considering. You can get offers of cheap or free equipment – who needs a double breastfeeding pillow and double pump ever again? (OK, unless you are a multiple, multiple mum.) You can form friendships with other members and be put in touch with other pregnant parents in the area – it's how we met (we were paired as 'twin buddies' by a local group as we both had older sons). They often have Facebook groups where you can post anything and everything, even at 2 a.m. when you are turning in bed for the eleventh time only to realise your bladder needs emptying *again*. Partners often have their own groups and outings as they may need their own support. They tend to have much more hands-on involvement and learning tips, or just sympathetic ears from people who have 'been there' can be just as important for them.

If you feel like you're not a 'group' sort of person then online support may be a better option for you. But try to be open-minded: getting out of the house is an important step and twin groups provide an easy, regular and welcoming opportunity.

Social media and parenting websites are great sources of free advice, support and friendship – at the time of writing, Facebook groups such as *Britain's Parents of Twins*, *Marvellous Multiple Mums*, *Dads of Twins*, *Twins (and more)* and *Pregnant with Twins* were all active and useful. Local community websites and Facebook groups may also be invaluable for sourcing cheap or free equipment.

Organisations – twins' organisations such as Twins Trust or Twins UK or Multiple Births Foundation are also worth joining. They have great reviews on equipment, and a huge number of articles, booklets and resources for anything from feeding to sleep to buggies to schools. Twins Trust also offers discounts on lots of different things including holidays, clothes and essential items for the home, and their monthly newsletter *Multiple Matters* is a good read with insights into the many different challenges and joys along the way.

Twins Trust runs Twinline, which is a listening and emotional support service that is free and confidential for all parents of twins, triplets and more in the UK. It is staffed by trained volunteers who are parents of multiples, and you do not need to be a member of Twins

Trust to use it. Twinline is open Monday to Friday from 10 a.m. to 1 p.m. and from 7 p.m. to 10 p.m. on 0800 138 0509. There is also an email address you can use which can be found through Twins Trust's website.

Twins Trust also has a team of twelve National Childbirth Trust-accredited peer supporters who have all breastfed twins and can offer mother-to-mother information and support to families who wish to breastfeed their twins, triplets or higher multiples. You can contact a peer supporter by email who will then call or email you back. (The email address at the time of writing this book is: breastfeedingsupport@twinstrust.org)

Join or sign up to some of these groups and, alongside this book, you'll get off to a good start.

ANTENATAL COURSES

If this is your first pregnancy, start with the free hospital antenatal courses, even if not twin-specific; you do not know at this stage what delivery you will have or how you will feed your babies. Breathing in labour, learning to latch, changing a nappy – this is all much-needed information that hospital midwives can provide. You'll start to hear terms such as 'trimester' which refers to different stages in your pregnancy, the first trimester being weeks 1–12, the second trimester 13–26 and the third 27 onwards. As there is a reasonable chance your twins will arrive early, try to book your antenatal course a little earlier than the suggested 30–32 weeks that is typical for singleton pregnancies. You may want to join another private antenatal course such as those organised by the National Childbirth Trust (NCT), as most mums report the start of great local friendships. For all antenatal courses, be prepared for some information not relevant to your likely experience (e.g. home births).

A specific antenatal course designed for parents of multiples is a bonus if you have one that runs near you. Most standard private or hospital-run antenatal courses do not cover twin-specific issues such as breastfeeding twins, how to manage in the early days with twins or even enough information on C-sections. Some hospitals run twin-specific courses but they are rare – it's much more likely you will find a private course by one of the twins' organisations or one such as Ella runs in North London. You may need to travel to attend one, which means you don't find the same network of local mums as you would at a course run close to home, but they are well worth the time and may include your first contact with a real-life twin mum.

Around this time, and with the help of information from your classes and hopefully some other twin parents, you may want to draw up your birth plan, which will document your preferences for how you give birth, what pain medication you would like, who you would like to be with you etc. This can be a very useful document to help articulate what you would like, but we would urge you to remain flexible and open-minded about how your pregnancy and birth may unfold and dictate some necessary changes to your plan.

***

Ella

Personally, when I am pushed to answer what antenatal courses to do, I say go for the free NHS ones and then if you are able to attend a twin-specific one do so. If the budget allows, and you want to, then attend a private general antenatal course on top for extra information and friendships, but this is not an absolute necessity. Why do I say this? Because being a parent of twins gives you an automatic entry into a community that those with singletons do not get. We have regular groups, we have Facebook groups, we have buddy systems – if you get involved you will find friends.

Louise

Having attended a non-twin-specific antenatal course over weeks for my son and a twin-specific course in a day for our twins, I would wholeheartedly recommend the twin-specific courses if you can possibly find one – the Twins Trust ones are very affordable. You will get more useful information in one day than in weeks of the other courses and at some general private courses may find yourself with confusing and upsetting information such as terrible tales of induction during natural births, which may be your hospital's highly recommended path for the delivery of your twins (for good reason).

***

BOOKS, READING AND HOMEWORK

We are firm believers in reading and preparation, especially with twins (hence this book). But finding out what to read is the hard bit when there is so much out there and everyone has an opinion.

As mentioned previously, Twins Trust and the Multiple Births Foundation have wonderful information online as well as booklets and pamphlets you can print out or send off for on specific topics.

General baby books

Books on having one baby will of course be useful – try *Your Baby Week by Week* by Simone Cave and Dr Caroline Fertleman (which was particularly popular amongst the twin mums we surveyed as it was precise to the week) or *Your Baby Month by Month* by Su Laurent. But there are tons of others; ask like-minded parent friends which they would recommend. Try, if you have a partner, to find a book for them to read alongside you, for example *Confessions of a Learner Parent* by Sam Avery (who also happens to be a twin parent!).

Breastfeeding

If you are thinking about breastfeeding and these are your first babies, it is essential to read up on this and prepare yourself. A book Ella rates highly is *What to Expect When You're Breastfeeding… And What If You Can't* by Clare Byam-Cook, and there is also an accompanying DVD which Louise found very useful even having breastfed her elder son successfully before her twins arrived. Another breastfeeding book with great reviews is *Mothering Multiples* by Karen Kerkhoff Gromada published by La Leche League.

Best Beginnings is a charity with fantastic online video clips and written material on breastfeeding, including twins. They have a DVD you can buy or you can view clips online. Another useful online resource is Dr Jack Newman's breastfeeding articles and videos (accessible via his website or on YouTube); he is a paediatrician in Canada who also runs a breast-feeding clinic. There are some excellent videos on latching and how to tell if your baby is feeding well.

Life as a twin mum

Happy Twin Mum by Kerri Miller – lovely account of Kerri's first year as a mum of twins, plus input from other mums, so it is well-rounded. Very helpful on the reality of premature twins and how to make your day work when you can't afford extra care.

Double Trouble: Twins and How to Survive Them by Emma Mahony – one woman's experience and recom-mendations.

Ready or Not... Here We Come! by Elizabeth Lyons – a humorous, honest book about the experience of hav-ing twins by an American mom. (Some of the practical advice is not relevant outside the US.)

Mother Ship by Francesca Segal – beautifully written account of one mother's experience of premature delivery of identical twin girls and their early days in neonatal intensive care.

PREGNANCY – WHAT ARE THE MAJOR DIFFERENCES?

This book is not going to cover everything to do with pregnancy and labour – there are many good general books for that and it's an enormous topic. But there are some important differences that having twins will mean for you.

WHICH HOSPITAL?

Soon into your pregnancy you may need to choose which hospital to have your babies at and where to go for all your scans and check-ups. You may not have a choice of hospitals but, if you do, some hospitals have a dedicated twins' team which usually means that you get to see the same midwife, doctor and ultrasonographer allocated for multiples at every visit (giving you great continuity and reassurance that they have had experience of twins). Don't worry if this isn't offered, but do ask if there are consultants and midwives who have experience of twins. If there are any complications you may be referred to another hospital or consultant. Generally, the larger the hospital, the more births they will have experienced, meaning you are more likely to come across staff who have a record of caring for twin mums and delivering twins.

BASIC PHYSICAL STUFF: YOUR BODY

As you may have already experienced, multiple pregnancy is usually accompanied by more nausea and morning sickness than the average singleton pregnancy. The usual cures of dry crackers before you get up, ginger tea or biscuits, rest and relaxation, small regular meals – and avoiding whatever triggers your nausea as much as possible – should work to some extent. (Louise found it helped to carry a tangerine on public transport and start peeling it under her nose if any of her fellow passengers were unavoidably triggering an attack.) There are some complementary therapies that may help, such as aromatherapy massage – but make sure the practitioner is aware you are pregnant. Some mums try the acupressure wrist bands that are often used for travel sickness and feel that they may help – they are pretty cheap and available to buy online. See your GP or midwife if the nausea is really limiting how much you are able to eat and drink as it is important that you stay hydrated and keep your strength up.

In a multiple pregnancy there is also more chance of back pain or hip pain, more trips to the loo and a general feeling of being tight and uncomfortable. Becoming aware of where the nearest – and most pleasant – public toilets are will stand you in good stead for many years to come!

EXERCISE

It's highly unlikely – but not impossible – that you will be able to continue your usual regular exercise very far into your pregnancy, so get used to taking things at a gentler pace. Do not start any vigorous new exercise routines in your pregnancy – just continue with whatever you were doing before, but listen to your body if you're getting very tired.

When you are past the first trimester, we recommend you start pregnancy yoga or Pilates to build up your strength and learn how to stretch and relax your body correctly. There are some great free videos online of pregnancy yoga if classes are too expensive or hard to get to.

If you are having severe pain walking, the hospital can refer you to a women's physiotherapist (or may refer you to pregnancy yoga or Pilates). It's pretty unavoidable when you reach your seventh and eighth month of pregnancy that walking to the shops and back will feel like a marathon, but please mention it to your midwives as there may be help they can offer.

Pelvic floor exercises

There is one set of exercises you must do during and after pregnancy – pelvic floor or Kegel exercises. The pelvic floor consists of layers of muscles that stretch like a hammock from the pubic bone (at the front of your pelvis) to the end of the backbone supporting the uterus, bladder, small intestine and rectum, all of which come under great strain in pregnancy and childbirth. A very common complaint during and after childbirth is urinary and stress incontinence (when you 'leak' urine on coughing, sneezing or laughing) and these exercises will help.

All pregnant women should do these exercises. It is just as important to do these exercises whether you are having a C-section or a vaginal birth. The real pressure on the pelvic floor is the weight of the babies, not the vaginal birthing process itself. By performing pelvic floor exercises, you can strengthen the muscles. This helps to reduce or avoid stress incontinence after pregnancy even if you are not suffering from stress incontinence now. Lots of pregnancy yoga classes will guide you through various different pelvic floor exercises but it's very simple to get started on your own – if you don't know how, search online for the latest NHS guidance, and the Pelvic Obstetric and Gynaecological Physiotherapy website has some leaflets to download. There are also apps being developed with reminders and exercises to follow.

***

Georgina

The online yoga was really helpful, just in your house and with a toddler, if you have twenty or thirty minutes. They had loads of prenatal stuff. I was pretty surprised at how fast my fitness levels totally deteriorated after six months… having some yoga helped me feel like not a total lump.

Jo

I developed lower back pain in my first pregnancy. Lots of pregnancy Pilates was really helpful during my pregnancy with the twins; I felt really strong by the time they were born. I was focused on having healthy babies and a healthy body at the end of the pregnancy – there weren't many pedicures and massages this time around.

Vic

One of the things that I really enjoyed during the pregnancy was going to pregnancy yoga because it just felt very grounding, like I was doing something really positive. I also met another person there who was having twins which was amazing in a room of singleton pregnancies and we're still friends now, we hang out together! The yoga was great but also that I met someone I could just talk about stuff and she lived around the corner from me, it was an absolute gift!

***

DIET

You may find that you want to eat vast amounts and in fact you should be eating more than usual (about another 600 calories a day), so don't worry about this. Soon you'll be too full of babies to fit much in anyway. Make sure you are eating healthily (complex carbohydrates such as wholemeal bread and porridge oats, fresh fruit and vegetables, lean protein) then go with your appetite. Protein is especially important in the second and third trimesters – an easy way to make sure you're getting enough is to swap your usual grande latte for a grande milk (maybe mix it up a little with a shot of hazelnut or vanilla occasionally).

Iron-rich foods are also very important as there is

a higher chance of you becoming anaemic during a twin pregnancy. It may even be worth taking a herbal iron supplement relatively early into your pregnancy (make sure it is suitable for pregnancy), as this will help with tiredness and help prevent anaemia without causing constipation. Your doctor will check iron levels in your second trimester as routine at which point you may be prescribed some (free) iron supplements.

Drink lots of water – dehydration can trigger early labour in the second and third trimesters, and if you're going to breastfeed you'll want to down pints faster than a student in freshers' week so it's a good habit to get into.

REST

Tiredness also seems to be greater for most twin mums, sometimes more so in the early months with a little break in the three-to-six-month period. Listen to your body and make sure you take rests when you need to. If you are working, try to seek out somewhere you might be able to rest and take a break if needed (not easy in the early days when your pregnancy may be a secret, we realise).

Later in the pregnancy you will have difficulties sleeping through frequent trips to the loo and plain discomfort, whether through sleeping on your side continuously to accommodate your bump or because somebody has stuck their foot in your ribs whilst someone else pushes down on your pubic bone. There are some great pregnancy pillows on the market that may help, but some mums just use ordinary pillows positioned between their legs and under their bump, for example, to help get comfortable.

Power napping in the day may become essential, and learning how to relax through meditation techniques is a good skill to pick up (sometimes taught at antenatal classes but there are lots of downloads and online resources on the topic).

MATERNITY WEAR

You're going to have a big bump that will need accommodation and will lift hemlines. If you have any hope of covering your bump after six months, tops need to be thigh length and dresses may need to be paired with leggings if you're uncomfortable exposing your legs above the knee. Invest in a pair of comfortable slip-on shoes by about the fifth month – trainers are great but no one wants to be tying laces in month eight. One less glamorous addition to your wardrobe is a support belt – great for the back and bump and may also provide a little coverage if your tops are creeping up and trousers slipping down!

But you don't need much to get you by, and if you have any smart occasions towards the end of your pregnancy your twin mum group may have some outfits they can lend you – it's unlikely you'll ever be that big again. Use the money saved to treat yourself to something post-birth (really comfortable pyjamas are possibly the best treat).

Try to wait as long as possible – week 32 at the earliest – before getting measured for nursing bras. Buy some with some stretch, as your milk-laden breasts may get larger than you could possibly imagine.

***

Alison

The clothes I wore when heavily pregnant were really different to the style and cut I needed afterwards. For example, when pregnant I wore stretchy/fitted dresses as my bump was nice and firm. The maternity trousers weren't comfy at all for me. But once I'd had the boys the dresses looked awful as my tummy was all wobbly and empty! So, I needed trousers and loose tops. But I didn't have many of those as I'd lived in dresses and couldn't find time or incli-

nation to get to the shops and ended up buying lots of volu-minous tops online – and sending most of them back!

***

STRETCH MARKS

You may get them; you may not. Some swear by creams and oils; others swear it's all genetic. Good luck.

WHEN TO FINISH WORK

Deciding when to finish work should be a decision taken between you and your midwives or doctors based on your occupation and health. General guid-ance would be around 32 weeks for someone with a desk job, but sooner than that if your job involves any sort of physical activity (some of the mums we spoke to saved up some annual leave to add to their mater-nity leave). Some of the twin mums we spoke to kept working until 36 weeks, but this was rare.

MEDICAL CONDITIONS

Your pregnancy can seem 'medicalised' in comparison to friends' or family members' experience with a sin-gleton pregnancy, especially if you're feeling well, but it is for good reason. Put simply, there *are* more complications when having two babies. You are (hopefully) not ill, but it's important that your pregnancy is monitored. Just keep asking and talking to the medical team about what they're doing, how you're progressing and make notes of any concerns between appointments so you have a good list to take in with you (easy to forget when you're surviving on very broken sleep due to six trips to the loo every night).

Medical complications include high blood pressure, pre-eclampsia, anaemia and gestational diabetes – the same conditions that can happen in any pregnancy are simply more likely with more babies. This is why your pregnancy will be officially 'high-risk' even if everything is going smoothly and you are feeling great (we hope). You will be offered more ultrasound scans as well as additional tests – for example, a glucose tolerance test for diabetes. For the medical team this is part and parcel of their daily work, but for you it is not, so, if you do not understand why something is being offered, ask and get it clarified. Lots of mums report having bleeds early on in their pregnancies which turned out to be nothing, but get any symptoms you're worried about checked out as soon as you can – medical staff should be understanding and sympathetic.

Towards the end of the pregnancy you are also

likely to develop Braxton Hicks contractions which are like 'practice' contractions: your bump will tighten but without the regularity and increasing intensity of labour contractions. At first these can be quite worrying as you may think you're going into early labour, but they should subside if you change your activity, take a bath, lie down or simply have a glass of water and a sit. If they do become more regular, or you have any other symptoms alongside them, seek medical assistance immediately.

BABIES' GROWTH

Commonly, there can be differences in growth between your babies and this may necessitate more monitoring; sometimes the term 'IUGR' (intrauterine growth restriction) might be used, which means one twin is growing too slowly. There may be a discussion about delivering the babies early if one is not growing well or the medical team is worried about the blood supply to one of the babies. They will offer you a steroid injection before delivery to boost the babies' lung strength and get them ready for life outside the womb.

PREMATURE DELIVERY

Try to be mentally prepared for the possibility of your babies arriving slightly earlier than planned. Around 60 per cent of twins will arrive before 37 weeks, with the average twin pregnancy lasting 35 weeks. Spontaneous premature labour can happen at any time and is more common with multiple pregnancies but it is still much more common to get to at least 30 weeks than to deliver before this. Interestingly, premature twins tend to cope better once outside the womb than singletons, needing shorter stays in neonatal care. Babies are resuscitated in the UK from 23 weeks of gestation and they averagely weigh 500 grams. Twenty-three weeks is very early and thankfully rare – these babies do have a hard time, need a lot of medical intervention and not uncommonly have difficulties that can be long-lasting, including disabilities.

It can be very difficult to take this all in if you go into very early labour – it is scary – but delivery can sometimes be delayed through bedrest and observation or stopped through medication. In most circumstances, the longer babies stay in the womb and develop, the more able they will be to cope with the outside world. However, if they are not getting the right nourishment, for example because of pre-eclampsia, and are growing too slowly, they may need to be delivered early and helped along their way in the neonatal unit. It will be a discussion between you and the medical team as to the best time to deliver the babies, to give them the best chance. Commonly, this is between 30 and 34 weeks for babies deemed to be at this kind of risk.

In general, it is likely that babies born before 34 weeks or babies who weigh under 2 kg will go to the special care baby unit (SCBU) or neonatal unit and will need some help with feeding and temperature regulation. Babies born before 30 weeks are likely to need help with their breathing. But, to state the obvious, all babies are different and it is hard to make generalisations about what will be needed at what time. If you do find yourself with premature twins, remember to ask lots of questions of the medical team to help you understand what's happening.

It is worth visiting the neonatal unit whilst you are pregnant so you can be prepared in the event of this scenario and it will not be so much of a shock. If you are not allowed to visit because of hospital policy, some hospitals have online videos to look at instead. You can also see some informative clips on the Best Beginnings website.

You may end up in hospital for weeks leading up to the delivery or on strict bedrest at home to help delay the babies' arrival. You will need a lot of support and friends around to help the time go quickly and keep happy; perhaps a rota of visitors, some good food and some box sets loaded onto a tablet – oh, and of course our book to read. Kerri Miller's book *Happy Twin Mum* has a really helpful account of her babies' time in the neonatal unit and special care, one to download if you find this may be a possibility for you. *Mother Ship* by Francesca Segal may also be helpful to understand the emotional highs and lows of a stay in neonatal care (keep a box of tissues by your side for that one).

It's worth noting that premature delivery does not necessarily mean a C-section and does not mean breastfeeding is not an option. We will come back to the topic in the chapters on those subjects.

***

Georgina

For me the birth was very dramatic, just because it was completely unexpected and early. My waters broke at 29 weeks and then we ended up in the hospital for eight days before they were born for monitoring. When labour came it was very, very fast, I didn't even think it was labour so the actual birth was an emergency Caesarean and it was pretty scary – the whole medicalised side of things. I was very scared of the epidural, having a big needle in my back. In theatre it was like a crazy Lady Gaga video, the things over the top of you and so many people and uniforms. And I really didn't know what the babies would look like because they were early. I had gone up to NICU, the intensive care unit, at 30 weeks as I wanted to be familiar with it but it was too emotional going inside. Then, when they were delivered, I heard them cry and that was a huge relief and they were whisked away to their incubators. Looking back on the whole procedure, I was so grateful to the medical team and thought they were amazing; I was so amazed at what they do.

***

ONE OR TWO PLACENTAS AND KEY ISSUES

If your twins share a placenta then they are identical. If you have a boy and a girl, then they will have two placentas and are not identical (this may seem obvious but people will ask you!). People often assume that if your babies have two placentas they are not identical; however, a third of same-sex twins who have separate placentas are identical – you can get a cheek swab test for free from the Multiple Births Foundation to know for sure.

In general, twins that share a placenta are at more risk of complications during pregnancy than those with their own placentas. If the twins also share the same amniotic (fluid) sac, that can be riskier still.

Twin to twin transfusion syndrome (TTTS)

Identical twins who share a placenta (monochorionic twins) are at risk of twin to twin transfusion syndrome, where there is an imbalance in their connecting blood vessels. This results in one baby (known as the recipient twin) getting more blood and nutrients and growing too big, putting a strain on his or her heart, and the other baby (known as the donor twin) receiving too little and growing too slowly. Importantly, the vast majority of twins who share a placenta grow normally. Almost eight out of ten monochorionic twins do not develop TTTS. However, TTTS can be very serious if it is not treated. Fortunately, treatment is successful in 90 per cent of cases. You will have regular ultrasounds to look for early signs of TTTS, usually every two weeks from 16 weeks to at least 24 weeks.

If TTTS is detected, it can be scary and worrying but there are good treatment options available. If there are any worries about TTTS developing, you will be referred to your nearest foetal medicine unit (doctors who specialise in looking after unborn babies and their mothers). The majority of cases will only require increased monitoring or scanning (there are some very helpful leaflets from Twins Trust on this). If the TTTS requires treatment then the foetal medicine team should discuss all the different options thoroughly with you. These include procedures such as draining amniotic fluid from the fuller sac to help correct the imbalance. In severe TTTS the specialist may be able to use a laser to seal off vessels in the placenta. This will stop the blood supply imbalance between your twins but does carry risks which the doctors will discuss with you. You will then be very closely monitored and may be advised to deliver the babies by planned C-section (there is a small risk of acute TTTS developing in labour itself) earlier than 36 weeks, which would be standard for monochorionic twins who do not have TTTS and are growing well. The delivery will need to take place in a hospital with a neonatal intensive care unit in case the babies need help once they are born.

It is hard to know what symptoms to report to doctors, especially in a first pregnancy, but if you are at risk and are concerned always mention it to your doctors or midwives. Symptoms for TTTS include feeling breathless, your tummy feeling tight and shiny and your abdomen getting noticeably larger (even in a twenty-four-hour period), and you must seek medical help urgently. The rapid increase in belly size often goes hand in hand with rapid increases in body weight, and other symptoms can include pain, tightness, or early contractions.

BEREAVEMENT

We wanted to mention this very tough and sad subject. During a small number of twin pregnancies, one may not survive. This may be picked up on a routine scan, but with the increasing frequency of early scans, for example after fertility treatment, more women are aware that, sadly, this has happened to them.

Much rarer is the loss of a twin later in pregnancy or at birth. Thankfully, this rate has been much reduced due to the close monitoring of twin pregnancies and the guidance to deliver twin babies a little earlier than singletons, alongside rapid advances in survival rates for premature babies.

If this happens to you, please don't be alone with your pain – it's a more common experience than people realise and others who have been through this are very willing to help. Twins Trust have a lot of guidance and support for this, as well as Child Bereavement UK.

There has also been a growing movement to signify babies who were once part of a multiple pregnancy or birth but have lost a twin or siblings by marking their cots in hospital with a purple butterfly. This is both to honour a lost baby and to inform other families and hospital professionals of the situation in a gentle and respectful way.

BABY (FOETAL) MOVEMENTS

Feeling your babies' movements is a sign that they are doing well. Most women begin to feel movements between 16 and 24 weeks. At first, it can feel like a kick, a flutter or a sort of pressing sensation. As the babies grow and space becomes tighter (usually in the second trimester compared to the third trimester for a singleton) the individual kicks, punches and jabs(!) are harder to feel as there is less room for gymnastics and instead you might feel these movements as more of a rolling or pressing sensation in the abdomen. Most twin mums find it hard to tell if the movement is twin one or twin two because the babies are so close to each other it can be very hard to work out whose arm or foot is stuck in your ribs!

There is no set number of movements you should feel. What is important is to get to know your own two babies' patterns of movement. Your babies will have periods of movement and periods of rest throughout your pregnancy, and the types of movements you feel, as explained above, may change as your pregnancy continues. But their movements should not slow down towards the end of pregnancy, so it is really vital for you to get to know your babies' normal pattern of movements. As their position inside changes less, you should be able to work out which is which (and both must keep moving).

If you notice any reduction or change in their pattern then get in touch with your midwife, health professional or maternity unit that day and seek their advice. It is very common that women come in and get checked out; this involves listening for the babies' heartbeats, carrying out an antenatal examination, having some monitoring for movements and maybe an ultrasound. In plenty of cases, it is reassuring that everything is as it should be and the babies are well and you will be allowed home. If you are worried again about reduced baby movements, even after this reassurance, it is still worth seeking medical advice again anytime up until delivery. It may be that your twins are so squished that it is becoming harder to detect their movements now, so don't immediately worry and think something concerning has happened, but call and get checked out to make sure everything is OK.

The health team will look very closely at both individual babies' growth, activity and the amount of amniotic fluid around them and also check for any discordant growth where one twin is growing faster than the other. If there is anything the midwife or doctor is concerned about, they should discuss it all with you fully and together work out a plan for ongoing monitoring and/or treatment.

WHAT'S IT REALLY LIKE?

Finding out you're having twins is an incredible feeling that can leave you full of so much excitement about what the future holds for your instant family. Reality bites, however, and, frankly, being pregnant with twins is a slog, particularly at the end. Save up the box sets, put your feet up and try to enjoy doing nothing as much as possible. Read books, join relevant Facebook groups, sign up for apps or do some online karaoke, whatever gets you through it. Do not worry about how many chocolate biscuits you're eating and try to stay gently active for as long as is comfortable. Try not to worry about what your stomach will look like afterwards; you might be one of the random lucky ones. Take pictures and marvel at your size and what an amazing job your body is doing supporting three hearts and three brains!

Healthwise, it's a lot to take in. A lot to worry about. A lot to get – tentatively – excited about. Frankly you'll be sicker, more tired and in more pain than most other pregnant women you've known and the last three months are endless. Try to put Google down (once in a while). Twins are more common now, and we are fortunate to have very high standards of medical care in the UK. But don't be afraid to ask questions and, remember, everyone has the same goal – two healthy babies and a happy, healthy mum.

Chapter 2: Preparing for the Birth

The current recommendations are that twins who share a placenta (and are therefore identical) will be delivered by 36 weeks and twins who have two placentas (who can be identical or non-identical) are delivered by 37 weeks because of the small increased risk of stillbirth if babies are delivered after that time. You can view the guidelines for yourselves online by searching for NICE, the National Institute for Clinical Excellence.

If you are having a planned C-section, the medical team will talk this through and set a date in line with these recommendations. If you are trying for a vaginal birth, then you will be offered induction if you have not gone into labour by the recommended time. You will usually have a discussion with your obstetrician around 32 weeks to talk through birth options and options for delivery.

Steroids will be offered to anyone delivering early or likely to deliver before 37 weeks. They come in the form of two injections for the mother. The drug crosses the placenta to mature the babies' lungs whilst in the womb. It works exceptionally well. Always ask about this if you go into early labour – it's important to get the steroids in early as they don't start to work immediately and so the longer they have to work before the babies are born, the more effective they are. This is something useful for your birth partner to remember – ask for the steroids!

But before we get into details, a word from the wise...

***

Jo

Don't focus too much on the birth process; they'll come out one way or the other and it is mostly beyond your control – you have to trust the people who are looking after you. What you really want is two healthy babies and there are other things you can focus on which are more in your control. I know very few people who had the birth they'd envisaged. Spend time with your partner doing nice things in the lead up to the birth – cinema, meals out – it'll be a while before you do this again.

***

BIRTH OPTIONS

You *do* have options, but realistically not as many as your friends who are having only one baby. A home birth or even delivery on a birthing unit is highly unlikely to be recommended or allowed – your delivery will most likely be on the labour ward. There is a more than 50 per cent chance of a C-section due to various factors from parental choice to medical advice. It often depends on the health of the babies and mother and also the position of the placenta and the first twin – twin one is the baby nearest the cervix and needs to be head down (cephalic) to attempt a vaginal delivery. The second twin's position is less likely to be a determinant for a C-section as the first's delivery will allow room for the second to manoeuvre (or be manoeuvred).

Vaginal delivery

More people will get involved at a vaginal birth than just a midwife, you and your birth partner – there will usually be more health professionals on hand, including more midwives and maybe a paediatrician and obstetrician. In labour, an epidural is most often recommended even if it is not essential for pain relief (you may disagree). The reason is that if twin one delivers but twin two is having difficulties, it helps to have an epidural in place if any medical intervention is needed in a hurry. This could mean an emergency C-section but more usually involves assisted delivery in the form of ventouse or forceps. The babies will still be able to be given to you for skin-to-skin (see next chapter for info on this) if they are well. Just because you have twins and it's high risk, you are still able to have a say in what happens after the birth. But if the babies are small or early then their health will come first and they may need to see the paediatrician before being handed to you for your first skin-to-skin contact.

You don't have two lots of contractions, just two lots of pushing which, once you've got the hang of it for the first, should be OK for the second (and placentas after that but, frankly, that will be a blur). Despite lots of fear of this, only 3 per cent of women have a vaginal birth for the first twin and a C-section for the second. If you would like to go for a vaginal birth remember to stay as active and upright for as long as you can. Do not be afraid of the epidural; it will wipe away the pain and may mean you can rest before the really hard work begins – the pushing. One of the mums we surveyed decided, in agreement with her consultant, not to have an epidural, but agreed to have a spinal block (like an epidural but less adjustable) if further intervention had meant it was necessary (it wasn't). This is unusual and this mother had given birth previously.

***

Jibecke

It was fine, it was my first and it was a natural delivery. When I started out I said, 'I'm not going to have an epidural,' which I did have in the end – they advised that as it was twins in case there was an emergency, and the second baby they had to take with ventouse. They wouldn't have been able to do that without the epidural so I'm pleased that I had it in the end. I'm glad that a friend of mine explained with an epidural you can adjust it, so I would recommend it to anybody so you can have it when you need it. It's not like a normal anaesthetic which is either off or on.

Louise

I was amazed when the consultant strongly recommended I go for a vaginal birth stating, 'I think these two will just pop out.' After a straightforward birth with our son, and a few viewings of a One Born Every Minute *twins special, I decided that I would go for it. I had two membrane sweeps which were a bit painful but worth it, as on the day of induction I just needed to have my waters broken (I was nearly 37 weeks) to trigger labour. My labour was much longer – the epidural gave me the chance to rest and everything slowed down – so I needed a syntocin drip to get things going. I found the midwives and consultants very sensitive to my decision to have a vaginal delivery.*

I had my waters broken just after I arrived in the morning. I had a small crisis around eight hours in when I was worried I was going to have a C-section after all and was wishing I'd just scheduled it like a normal person! But after twelve hours I was ready to give birth. They wheeled me into theatre – it was eleven-thirty on a Friday night and I don't think they were as confident as I was that I was going to push them out – and George arrived just before midnight, Alice just afterwards (yep, different birthdays).

I ended up with first-degree tears, no surgical intervention and felt in much better shape afterwards than after my first, who was born via a drug-free water birth.

***

C-section

If you have a C-section (as around 60 per cent of twin mums do), whether planned or not, it will be in theatre and you will usually be awake, with a spinal or epidural anaesthetic in place. You will have a screen so you don't see the operation itself and your birth partner will be present. Only in the rare event of an extremely quick emergency delivery (known as a 'crash section') will they give you a general anaesthetic so you will be asleep.

Everyone will try to make it special for you. Think about things you might want, such as the music that is playing in the theatre or whether you would like to dim the lights, or see the babies before the surgeon announces the sex. The babies will be there for you to see and hold – remember it is *your* delivery.

A Caesarean may not be the birth you planned, and it is hard to come to terms with that sometimes. Talk to people and understand what happened. When you are back to yourself, if you still have unanswered questions you can make an appointment with your obstetrician to ask them questions. But try to focus, if you can, on the babies and their health.

***

Eleanor

At the end of the day the most important thing was that they arrived safely. It wasn't the amazing childbirth story that you hear some people having – whether anyone actually has that. It was very clinical, no doubt about it. Would I change that? No.

Jo

I'd had a relatively difficult pregnancy with the twins. Hyperemesis [severe nausea, vomiting, weight loss and possibly dehydration] *triggered my thyroid gland to become overactive. I also developed abnormal liver tests. This meant I was monitored more closely during pregnancy. I had two months off work with the sickness (and 15 kg weight loss!) but started to feel better around 20 weeks. At our 20–week scan we were told there were subtle abnormalities with twin one which could all be nothing but may have indicated a chromosomal* [genetic] *abnormality. We had difficult discussions at that time about whether to have an amniocentesis* [a prenatal test that gives information about your baby's health from a sample of your amniotic fluid] *but decided against it due to the (small) risks of harm to either baby and the risk of going into early spontaneous labour. At around 28 weeks twin one developed IUGR* [intrauterine growth restriction] *and so needed* regular scans to ensure I didn't need to be induced. This was an incredibly stressful time and because someone different did my scan each fortnight and I was transferred temporarily to another doctor I found it hard to fully trust the team looking after me.

My son Danny, who at this stage was just eighteen months, was born by emergency Caesarean section after being induced for four days and never establishing labour. I was therefore adamant that I wanted a planned Caesarean section for the twins in a controlled environment in the middle of the day. The consultant looking after me was happy with this and it was booked for the day before I turned 37 weeks. We were due to move house that same week (poor planning) so I was distracted by packing and change of address forms.

But the morning of their birth and how I felt will never leave me. I said goodbye to my nearly two-year-old, who trotted off happily to the playground with my mum. At that point in time I honestly thought I would never see him again (as I was convinced I would die in the operating theatre) and was putting all my energy into hiding how terrified I felt from him. We had no idea what the sex of our twins was and if they would be healthy, particularly given the issues surrounding twin one.

The removal men arrived shortly after and whilst I gave them instructions my husband disappeared for an hour (I've never really found out where he went – I think the stress was unbearable). We walked to the hospital and arrived at 13:15 (fifteen minutes later than asked – we'd just missed the consultant, who'd come to the ward to see me) and things thereafter happened very quickly. The nurse told me I hadn't shaved 'down below' properly which I was mortified about but I couldn't see a thing and it didn't occur to me to ask anyone else to do it! I hadn't seen beyond my bump for months! I remember walking to the operating theatre and having the epidural put in, which was pretty uncomfortable and makes your legs feel like lead. Then two men had to lift my legs onto the table as I couldn't move them.

I kept telling myself that the pain and indignity was nothing compared with what it would be like if I had had a vaginal delivery. The lighting in the operating theatre was very bright and you can't see a great deal as your bump is in the way. But the anaesthetists were lovely and chatted away to me and before I knew it there were lots of people in the room and the consultant was holding up my first little daughter, who was bellowing and promptly urinated everywhere. Jessie was born at 14:33 weighing 2.1 kg and Hannah followed at 14:35 weighing 2.3 kg. Hannah was much quieter and needed a bit of oxygen for a few minutes but I had a quick cuddle with both of them and then they were checked by the paediatricians whilst I was sewn up. I remember that bit taking what seemed like ages – probably in reality it took around thirty minutes – and I was just impatient to have a proper look at them. We then went into the recovery room where I could do skin-to-skin, feed them and stare adoringly at them. After what seemed like months of worrying and uncertainty they were finally here and perfect and we couldn't have been happier. And we went home two days later to our new home!

Katie

To be honest, I originally wanted a natural birth and was going to until about a week before, and was sort of disappointed and sort of relieved as the decision was taken away. It was a bit daunting going into a room with twenty people; even though everyone's very nice it did feel a bit like having an operation. Then one moment we were chatting to the anaesthetist about the effects of penicillin and then suddenly there was the first baby. It was all very quick and very sort of out of control. What was nice afterwards was in the recovery room when the midwife brought the babies to me and put them on my boobs, which was good because then they started feeding and it was nice to know that I could do *it. It wasn't plain sailing after that but the knowledge that they could suck just meant it could work.*

***

As we've mentioned above, it is likely with twins that you will have more medicalisation and a higher chance of a C-section. We hope that if you have those expectations and know this information beforehand then it might be easier for you to come to terms with the nature of your delivery – and lots of mums we spoke to who had C-sections (especially planned ones) had very positive experiences. Recovery is usually fine, and often not as bad as you think it will be. Moving and feeding can be harder, no way around that, but you can plan for how you might get around these things. Ella had an emergency Caesarean for her son and a planned Caesarean for her twins – her top tips for recovery are: 1) peppermint tea for any tummy pain; 2) Fybogel for your bowels; and 3) mobilise and sit up as much as possible.

It is usually a two-night stay post C-section, and the medical team may want to monitor you on the open bay in the postnatal ward for a few hours before you are well enough to move into a side room, if this is an option.

POSTNATAL CARE IN HOSPITAL

Do ask if there will be any side rooms or amenity rooms for your postnatal care. The hospital may well have these available for booking privately and this may be covered by medical insurance if you have it. The hospital may let you have a side room free of charge since you will need an extra pair of hands at night and this more easily allows someone to stay with you – but this is not at all guaranteed. If you are in an open ward, some hospitals will let your partner stay in a chair by your bed but most do not and may have strict visiting hours.

Prepare yourself to stay in for five days after the birth – regardless of how the birth goes – to ensure the babies are feeding properly. This is an estimate but get yourself mentally ready for being in for this length of time, until the doctors and midwives are happy with you, the babies' feeding and their weight. Finally, if you feel you need to stay longer, ask for an extra day to get your strength and confidence up – a few of the mums we interviewed did and all the hospitals were understanding and accommodating. From talking to many parents, we are aware that postnatal care and breastfeeding support can vary between hospitals, especially with regard to their twin expertise and time they can devote to helping you. We would advise planning ahead to get some help whilst you are there from partners, friends or relatives (especially for single parents).

EQUIPMENT

After all that medical talk, let's get down to some serious shopping. Intimidating – the volume, the expense – and enjoyable – all those little outfits! The first thing to remember is that hand-me-downs and second-hand (e.g. Gumtree, eBay, Preloved) are absolutely your friends. Whilst most of us will want to buy and carefully wash those very first outfits and blankets you'll bring the babies home in, most items are used so little in the first year, and are very easily washable. It's really worth keeping an eye out a few months ahead for second-hand Moses baskets, cots, bouncers and clothes, but do remember you'll need new mattresses. It's also ecologically sound to reuse rather than buy new, which may help assuage your guilt at the amount of disposable nappies you're bound to get through (twin mums using real nappies are out there and deserve instant OBEs for services to the environment). Twin groups are often full of mums happy to give away breastfeeding pillows and other items to other twin mums, so another good reason to join. You may also be lucky and receive gifts from friends and family. A good tip is to keep the original boxes and don't take anything out of the box unless you're absolutely sure you're going to use it – you can then sell things on more easily.

Before you start panic-buying, do remember that there are approximately five days in the year in the UK when shops aren't open and you need very little to start with. Don't panic; it really is OK if all you've bought by your thirtieth week are two coordinating cardigans that won't fit them for about a year. Someone with a list will be able to equip you very quickly should the need arise. Our first list is important, however – the hospital bag – and it is important to get it ready earlier than for a singleton pregnancy. All other items can definitely wait a few weeks or can stay in friends' lofts whilst you (watch someone else) paint the nursery.

ADDITIONAL FINANCIAL SUPPORT

Now is definitely the time to wise up about what government benefits are available to you – the key ones being child benefit, maternity pay and maternity allowance. At the time of writing, every first-time mother of twins can claim a Sure Start maternity grant

– a one-off payment of £500 – but this must be applied for within the eleven weeks prior to the birth or three months after (which parents can miss, especially in the frantic times of a premature birth). Dependent on your circumstances, you may also qualify for additional financial support from the government, such as tax credits (you may qualify for more once you have children) and childcare for older children. Check out the childcare and parenting section of the government benefits site (www.gov.uk/expenses-and-benefits-childcare), plus websites such as Working Families and Twins Trust will have further advice on what support you may qualify for.

HOSPITAL BAG – PACK ESSENTIALS BY 28 WEEKS

For you:

Essentials:

Hospital notes

Maternity pads (for your blood flow post birth, known as 'lochia' – heavy-flow sanitary pads with wings with a maternity pad stuck on top work well for extra security)

Big, high-waisted, tummy-hugger knickers – ones

you don't mind throwing away afterwards (you can buy disposable knickers but they can be a bit papery)

Hi-energy food such as glucose tablets, flapjack bars, cereal bars

Bottle of water (and possibly a bottle of squash if you get bored of a lot of water)

Nightwear – large, old t-shirts, old nightgowns (colours that don't show up wet patches, i.e. grey marl not advised)

2 x jogging bottoms and t-shirts/comfortable, roomy clothes to go home in

Mobile phone and charger (or wristwatch and camera)

Something easy to read

Notebook and pens (to note down questions, when feeds were and with which baby)

Hairbrush, hairbands, comb

Slippers or flip-flops (good for the shared shower)

Toiletries (shampoo, conditioner, face wash, body wash, creams, deodorant, face cloth)

Pocket mirror

Lip balm, facial wipes, maybe water spray, mini-fan for labour

Antibacterial wipes and gel

Toothbrush/paste

***

For breastfeeding:

Maternity bras or tops

Nursing cover (although you might not care in the early days and a muslin will do the job)

Lanolin cream (pure lanolin to prevent and heal cracked nipples – smother it on after every feed and then smother some more)

Breast pads (disposable are fine, washable can also work and can be more comfortable)

Breastfeeding book/leaflets with advice, numbers to call

***

For bottle feeding:

Starter pack of formula, bottles, teats (see below for more details on kit to have at home)

***

Optional:

Clear honey to dilute in warm water (if you have an epidural then the anaesthetist will want you to stay on clear fluids only – honey in warm water is a good alternative way to get some sugar. Also, many

women don't feel like eating in labour, and honey
and water is a good alternative if you can't face food)

Hot water bottle – good to have for back pain

TENS machine (if you want to try one)

Dressing gown

Towel (dark-coloured) – the hospital will provide
towels but not usually terribly luxurious

Earplugs – some people want to use these as it can be
hard to sleep on an open bay, but you must still be
able to hear your own babies all the time

Pillows – feeding pillow, V-neck pillow, your own
normal pillow with a fresh pillowcase (nice to have
something that smells of home)

***

For babies:

Newborn sleepsuits (six per baby) – consider at least
two 'tiny baby' for smaller babies. Check the weight
that they are designed for (it will sometimes be mentioned on the label, other times on the website).
Usually tiny baby is up to 3 kg/7 lb, which is big for
a newborn twin – average twin birth weight is 2.4
kg/5 lb 4 oz.

Vests (six per baby) – include two tiny baby size

Hats (two per baby)

Gloves/mittens (two per baby)

Nappies – one pack of newborn, one pack of micro nappies

Vaseline

Cotton wool pads

Nappy sacks

Blankets – swaddle blankets/receiving blankets or large muslins

4 x small muslins

Snowsuits or coats (plus hats) if cold weather

Car seats to go home

***

Optional:

Soothers/dummies – possibly not necessary in the immediate post-birth phase

***

Partner's bag:

Phone and charger (or camera, etc.)

Magazines, books, notepad and pen for your questions

List of people to call/text

Clothes and toiletries (one night's worth – fresh t-shirt and a toothbrush/paste will probably do it)

Snacks and drinks (ostensibly for the partner, but never

a mistake to make sure some of the new mum's favourite treats are in there too)

***

Optional:

Favourite local takeaway menus (she wants sushi the night after delivery – SHE GETS SUSHI)

***

Additional handy tips for the hospital bag

Make sure you have some Vaseline for the meconium nappies (meconium is the tar-like poo that babies produce in the first few days). Once you have cleaned the meconium away with water and cotton wool pads – more efficient than cotton wool balls – then you can pat dry and use the Vaseline over their bottom and do up the nappy. The next time your baby poos, the meconium will slide off instead of having to be scraped off like tar! Once they are on milk, the poos will change to a yellow mustardy colour. Initially, it is recommended not to use wipes because the babies' skin is so sensitive (although water wipes are OK) but after a couple of weeks you could try a wipe and see if your babies' skin can tolerate them.

For your own digestive system, consider packing a

snack in your hospital bag such as prunes or dried apricots that will help nature take its course through your system. Your first poo after birth is quite an important event and you'll be grateful for anything that aids transit.

Eye mask (with optional lavender essential oil) – Louise found this invaluable when she had a week's stay in the hospital when her first son was in NICU (neonatal intensive care unit) and then special care. It helped her sleep through the hospital hubbub and then the light of the UV bed her son was under (for jaundice). Lavender is generally good for relaxation and can be dropped onto the eye mask or pillow.

If you are generally someone who wears make-up, you may soon not be (Louise gave up). If you continue, you might want to consider waterproof mascara (and remover) due to the amount of hormonal and happy sobbing you may be doing.

WHAT TO GET FOR THE HOUSE? HOW MUCH?

1 x double buggy with rain cover
2 x foot muffs or pram blankets if cold weather
2 x car seats and 2 x Isofix bases (speak to a reputable shop such as Halfords or John Lewis about various

car seat options and configurations. If you need three car seats across the back, ask on the multiple forums what other parents have done with your model of car – but remember Isofix bases can be secured with seatbelts or the car's Isofix points.)

2 x slings

12 x newborn and tiny baby vests

12 x newborn and tiny babygros/sleepsuits

2 x hats

2 x cardigans

4 x socks (you will get given tons of these, more than you will ever need)

2 x snow suits or coats (weather dependent)

1 x cot or 2 x cots or 2 x Moses baskets

Cot divider

4 x sheets and cellular blankets (the holey ones)

1 x baby monitor (get one which shows the room temperature as well)

1 x changing mat (two is better – see below, Top Equipment Tips)

72 x newborn-size nappies (to get you started)

1 x nappy disposal bin (a bin with a lid is good enough)

2 x big bags of cotton wool pads

1 x big box baby wipes (i.e. about twelve packs – most mums will use them after the first few weeks,

plus they are excellent at cleaning baby-related stains from most fabrics)

1 x packet nappy bags (don't bother using them if the nappy is just wet and not soiled)

1 x nappy cream (or two if you have two changing mats) – Sudocrem, Metanium and Bepanthen are all good brands

8 x standard muslins plus a couple of really big ones (these are great for lots of jobs – swaddling, covering up when feeding, covering prams)

4 x towels (the ones with hoods are cute but not strictly necessary)

Soft hairbrush

Baby nail clippers or scissors

First-aid kit

***

Breastfeeders:

1 x breastfeeding pillow/V-pillow

1 x tube of lanolin cream

2 x nursing bras (fitted before delivery in a store) or soft nursing tops

1 packet of breast pads

Optional but strongly advised:

Double breastfeeding pump (see information below)

Optional:

Nipple protectors (they come in different sizes)

***

Bottle feeders:

8 x feeding bottles and teats (newborn teats and stage
   1, large bottles are fine and will last longer)
Bottle-cleaning brush
Formula (stage 1)
Formula container
Steriliser – steam/microwave or cold water (two if pos-
   sible)
2 x thermal bags for bottles
8 x bibs
A spare kettle
Thermos flask

***

Highly recommended but not essential at first:

4 x sleeping bags (only use these once the babies are
   around 3 kg/7 lb)

2 x baby bouncing chairs

4 x dummies (optional, useful to have)

2 x baby bath chairs (and a bath mat)

1 x large changing bag

Changing table/unit or a table (to avoid bending over all the time and hurting your back)

Play mat 1 x large or 2 x small

Outdoor outfits for babies, more socks, hats, etc. – but worth holding back if you can resist it as often people will buy these for you or hand them down to you

TOP EQUIPMENT TIPS

Two change mats – if you have an upstairs or a large one-floor living space, set up two changing stations complete with nappies, cotton wool, cream and changes of clothes. You want to minimise unnecessary toing and froing and up and down stairs or even between rooms.

Baby clothes – get some tiny baby or early baby clothes, in case your twins are small, as well as newborn (and, as indicated, have a mixture in your hospital bag). These clothes will be worn for a matter of days so do not be proud about getting these second hand – some will have never been worn, others will be as good as new – but we understand you may want their 'going home' outfit to be brand new.

Nappies – Pampers Micro nappies (smaller than newborn) for the early days are great. Our babies were all healthy weights and the newborn nappies were still big on them. You probably won't need many of these, however, maybe just two packs will do.

Bouncers – lots of different versions to suit budgets but BabyBjörn bouncers are incredible (though expensive). They fold flat and can be transported easily to a friend's house. They have three levels so the highest one can be used if your baby is vomity or has reflux after feeds, and they are very easy to keep clean. There is a good second-hand market for these.

Bottles – most people recommend at least six bottles per child and a very good steriliser, e.g. a microwave one. If you get second-hand bottles, buy new teats. If you're planning on breastfeeding, it's still worth buying a couple of bottles to have in the house for expressed milk or emergencies.

Breastfeeding equipment – a double breastfeeding pillow is recommended by most mums, who often pass theirs on for free to other mums (covers are washable). For breastfeeding you may need a V-shaped long pillow as well, which are available from lots of different shops e.g. Argos, John Lewis. Some mums do get by with a collection of pillows and cushions but it's worth trying one designed for the job.

Medical grade lanolin (commonest brand is Lansinoh) or coconut oil for cracked and sore nipples, which pretty much all mums get at the beginning. (Any unused makes great lip balm.)

A double breastfeeding pump is useful but very expensive. You could possibly find a second-hand one and sterilise it. You can also rent these online (they arrive the next day) and whilst in hospital you can use their pumps, so if you need one and don't have one, don't worry. A single breast pump is cheaper but takes double the time. Expressing can be very useful to build up your milk supply from the early days or if your baby is in the neonatal unit. Later on, it will mean you may be able to leave the babies with someone else or delegate night feeds. Some hospitals may lend these to you – please ask, especially if money is an issue.

Feeding bras, tops – you can get measured a couple of weeks before delivery but we would also suggest buying 'bra-like' stretchy supportive nursing tops to start with, as you have no idea quite how humongous your boobs will get or how long you will feed for. Cotton is best as easier to boil wash in case of fungal infections (more on that joy later). For those long-term pumpers, expressing bras allow you to be totally hands-free, and come highly recommended from those who have needed them.

Changing bag – a nice twin changing bag is lovely but not essential – a decent waterproof rucksack with lots of different pockets is probably better for the job – but it can be a nice present.

A pram – so many options and opinions. There are good buggy reviews on Twins UK or Designed for Twins or Twins Trust. The main questions are – side by side, or one in the front and one at the back? Do you want a travel system where you can pop on the car seats or not? Does it fit through your front door? Can you fit it in your hall? If you have a car, does it fit in the boot at all? Does it allow space for anything else? Most importantly, how much is it and what is your budget? Try to go to a nursery showroom and try some out; go to a twins new mums and bumps meet-up and see what everyone else is driving and recommending. The most popular brands at the time of writing are Baby Jogger, Bugaboo, iCandy and Mountain Buggy. Remember to work out the additional costs for the car seats and bases and any adaptors you need. Bassinets for the first few months are optional and often available in very good condition second-hand, although you will need to get new mattresses. Triple buggies do exist but try eBay as they cost a fortune. You might be better off trying out a buggy board for an older one or double buggy/sling combination before you invest.

***

Alison

My recommendation would be to buy the first buggy second-hand as the 'stacker' one is best when they are tiny (in my opinion) – but as soon as they're sitting up in the buggy this seemed too small and we outgrew it. I got a side-by-side buggy when they were six months and think it's fab. That was worth buying new as I'm using it for a lot longer, up to three years for this one versus just six months for the first one.

***

Slings – the only 'twin sling' we have seen consistently recommended is the 'Weego', but it's worth chatting to your local twin mums and going to a sling library. We both used fabric or BabyBjörn slings when a second person was around, or just one if one baby was unsettled and we needed to be hands-free for something else.

Beds – all mattresses should be new and not second-hand. Twins can share a cot initially, or two Moses baskets or two cots. People find Moses baskets very handy as they are portable. If they share a cot from the beginning they usually sleep widthways, feet to the side bars, until they get too long.

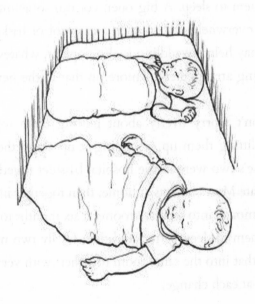

After this, you can move them so they are at either end of the cot, with feet to the end bars. You can get a cot divider to prolong the time before you need to get a second cot/cotbed, and this is useful if they start annoying each other at night by rolling on top of one another. A cotbed will last longer than a cot but takes up more space. Another alternative to a second cot or cotbed could be a travel cot with a thicker mattress as a temporary measure, but watch your back if you have to bend down a lot.

Twins tend to like closeness (as they were in the womb); it often helps with them feeling secure and for them to sleep. A big open cot can sometimes feel a bit overwhelming, so even a carrycot or basket in a cot may help. Swaddling is also popular, whatever the sleeping arrangement – more on that in the next section.

Don't worry overly about putting them together or splitting them up or mixing it up along the way. Louise's two were in the hospital bassinet together, in separate Moses baskets at home, then together in a cot, then moved into separate rooms at six months to try to get them to sleep better, and then finally two months after that into the same room together, with very little upset at each change.

HOWEVER, PLEASE FAMILIARISE YOURSELVES WITH THE GUIDELINES ON

SUDDEN INFANT DEATH SYNDROME
(SIDS, ALSO KNOWN AS COT DEATH) AND
FOLLOW THEM. FOR THE MOST
UP-TO-DATE GUIDANCE CHECK WITH THE
LULLABY TRUST, WHICH PROVIDES
EXPERT ADVICE ON SAFER SLEEP FOR
BABIES AND A PARENT SUPPORT LINE.
SAFE SLEEP ADVICE, TO REDUCE THE
RISK OF SIDS, INCLUDES:

Placing your baby on their back to sleep, in a cot in the
same room as you, for the first six months.

Not smoking during pregnancy or breastfeeding, and
not letting anyone smoke in the same room as your
baby.

Not sleeping in the same bed as your baby if you
smoke, drink or take drugs or are extremely tired, if
your baby was born prematurely or was of low birth
weight.

Never sleeping with your baby on a sofa or armchair.

Using a firm, flat, waterproof mattress in good condition.

Not letting your baby get too hot.

Keeping your baby's head uncovered. Their blanket
should be tucked in no higher than their shoulders.

Placing your baby in the 'feet to foot' position, with
their feet at the end of the cot or Moses basket.

Breastfeeding if you can.

Using a dummy when putting a baby down to sleep could reduce the risk of SIDS (once breastfeeding has been established).

This is important advice given out by the NHS and is readily available on the NHS website or from your midwife. Putting the babies together in a cot is not a risk factor for SIDS but it is not recommended that they share a Moses basket due to the risk of overheating.

GENERAL BUYING ADVICE

As well as all the second-hand options, there are other ways to save money. Remember, as a pregnant woman with two babies on the way, you are a very valuable customer and they want you for years to come, so take advantage – never buy anything without first searching for a discount code.

Join the baby clubs online to get various discounts, vouchers and free samples – most of the major supermarkets and brands run these (but do get ready for a deluge of emails and stuff through the post). Lots of websites do big discounts for your first purchase, so make sure it's a big one to take full advantage.

Twins Trust has some great discounts for baby gear, which is another great reason to join.

Bulk buying – some people love Costco for bulk buys, others swear by Amazon Prime and Subscribe & Save. There are also often good deals on nappies on the online shopping services, so look out and buy ahead.

Own brands – for nappies, wipes, basic clothes and linens, many people give excellent reports of the larger supermarkets' own products and they may save you literally hundreds of pounds over the next couple of years.

PLANNING AHEAD FOR SUPPORT

During the last few months of pregnancy it's worth setting up support for the first six weeks at home, and beyond that if possible. This may mean phoning friends for advice or sympathy, knowing when support groups are happening near to home, asking friends and family to volunteer their time or handle certain tasks for you and seeking extra pairs of hands from organisations. For those that can afford it, paying for help with the house or other children can be a big help too – and now would be a good time to interview or check that you would be happy having that person around when you might be feeling at your most vulnerable. It is essential you think about it now as you won't have the energy or ability to make good decisions or ask the right questions of the right people in the days and weeks directly after the babies arrive.

One easy thing to do is online grocery shopping – you can download your supermarket of choice's app and do this at any time of day or night. If you don't already do your grocery shopping online and have the means to, try to set this up beforehand. It makes life easier and the person who deliver will even unpack your shopping for you (worth a tip). If online shopping doesn't work for you for financial or other reasons, rest assured, most mums we spoke to reported the upside of a trip to the supermarket being a great reason to get out of the house.

ON THE PHONE

Make a note of the following phone numbers and keep it somewhere sensible:

Your midwives

Your health visitors (you may not find this out until after the babies are born, don't worry)

Your GP

Twins Trust Twinline – open Monday to Friday

from 10 a.m. to 1 p.m. and from 7 p.m. to 10 p.m. on 0800 138 0509 (freephone)

Cry-Sis – support for crying, sleepless and demanding babies – open seven days a week from 9 a.m. to 10 p.m. – 08451 228 669

Have a look at the new parent-matching apps such as Peanut and Mush, you might find some other parents with babies the same age as yours in your area and details of local meet-ups. Whilst meeting other new twin mums is wonderful to have someone to relate to, with the right friends who are mums of singletons you have another pair of free hands whilst you're out and about.

IN THE LOCAL AREA

Make a calendar of local events such as community baby and breastfeeding support groups and baby classes such as those at the local children's centre, library or church hall – you probably won't make them for some time after the singleton mums, but it's worth knowing when they are. One day when you are feeling isolated and need to get out, you can have a look and have somewhere to go.

Know when your local twins' group meets up as well – it really will be the best place for that first visit out of the house as you will be welcomed extremely warmly by all the other mums who have been there and understand why all three of you might be crying and why you're still wearing pyjamas under your jeans.

HELP AT HOME – IN MULTIPLE FORMS

With hindsight, neither of us felt we worked out our childcare as well as we could have done, which certainly contributed to Ella's exhaustion and ill health in her girls' early days. Your options will depend on your own personal circumstances, finances, family involvement, number of children and health of the twins. But here are a few common tips we wish we had known.

Homestart is a charity covering most of the UK that can send a volunteer to your house for three hours once a week to help you out with your children. They are trained and DBS checked. You cannot leave the babies with them but those extra pairs of hands will be a help. Contact your local branch to find out more. If you feel you don't get on with the person they send you, ask for another one! It's OK.

Some colleges used to send their trainee nannies out to work in placements with newborn twins but this has pretty much stopped now unfortunately. It is still worth checking to see if anything has changed by finding out which local college has nanny or childcare courses and speaking to the course organisers.

Friends and family – never refuse help that is on offer but make it specific. Never be shy to ask for household help rather than help with the children. Speak to relatives who are offering to stay or come over regularly to help, and explain the kind of help that you will need. If you have a relative over, they do not need to be sitting and holding the babies whilst you make them tea. A VISITOR IS NOT A GUEST BUT A HELPER. This is a crucial point. Babies who are fed and comfortable hopefully will sleep and then you can rest and the visitors can help around the house. It can be hard getting this point across to mothers or mothers-in-law but do try to talk it through with them whilst pregnant – show them this page if that will help. The basic message is, you will need help around the house and not just with the babies.

Cooking – one of the best things that anyone can do for you. A group of Ella's friends got a dinner rota together and fed her family for two weeks – amazing. Friends can do freezer cooking beforehand and if you have a small freezer could even store it for you.

Housework – if at all possible, although probably unrealistic, but practically this should not be your job, especially if you are breastfeeding twins or recovering from surgery. Practise saying 'the bathroom' when someone asks, 'Is there anything I can do to help?'

Older children – usually everyone, including partners, will want to take your older child or children off your hands. That is helpful and kind but it is not always what you or they want – so ask them instead to help you spend time together when you need to.

Allowing you to go for walks – you will feel housebound so it's important you get out of the house as soon as you can. If your helper is not someone who is a natural housekeeper or cook, ask them to accompany you for a walk with the babies if you're still feeling a bit nervous about being out with them on your own, or even sit with the babies whilst you have a ten-minute stroll around the block.

Allowing you to nap – you may want to talk to everyone about how wonderful your babies are, or give them the full birth story blow-by-blow, but you do need rest. It can be incredibly helpful just to know someone is watching the babies whilst you get fifteen minutes of lying down on the bed upstairs in the quiet. During this time, try not to obsessively check how many likes your latest picture on Facebook has got.

***

Alison

Don't overbook visitors, just try with a few at first to see how you cope. I found them quite overwhelming and only wanted a certain kind of friend (low maintenance and with lots of initiative in helping!).

***

PARTNER'S PARENTAL LEAVE

We recommend you use your partner's parental leave carefully and usefully. If you have close family staying with you to help straight after the birth, an option could be to split the leave up: a week after the birth and a week once your relative has gone. A good tip is to not have everyone helping at once in the early days and then nobody. Try to ensure you can have family help over the longest period, if you possibly can.

If your babies are in NICU or SCBU for even a week, it will be worth your partner going back to work until the babies arrive home and you no longer have nurses and midwives looking after you and them.

***

Vic

Ali took two weeks' parental leave then she took another week off which was amazing – she's totally amazing, we totally did this together, it was our decision, both our first family. Then my parents came down for three weeks so I feel really lucky that I had six weeks with live-in care and I don't know how I would have coped without it. I was in the feeding regime of every three hours and every feed was breast and then bottle. I was so weak it would take two hours to feed them and feeding them every few hours meant you just had to grab half an hour's sleep when you could! I just needed people to hold them and look after them and just pass them to me. And you're just learning how to feed, how the latching works. They would have had to go on to bottles if I didn't have that help.

*****

SINGLE PARENTING

If you are twin parenting on your own we salute you – and want to reassure you that you can do this. Setting up support networks and making sure you can call on people to help is clearly extra important for you. Try to spend some time with a twin mum who has small babies before yours arrive, it'll be less of a culture shock when yours are here! Make sure you call Homestart and explain your situation to them, chat to your health visitor and see what support they can help you find. If you have financial worries, charities such as

Gingerbread and Family Lives have some great advice and may be able to offer practical support. (But if you do have any spare funds then paid help such as cleaning or babysitting would be well worth the investment.)

Many of the mums with partners practically handle everything the babies bring, and survive, but what they have is the ability to walk around the block and have a chat about how hard their day has been. Think about who your daily phone call can be with, are there any neighbours who could sit with you and have a cup of tea (and watch the babies whilst you pop to the loo!)? Feeling isolated in the early weeks and months is very hard, so push yourself to get out of the house – fresh air will be good for you and the babies.

Do sign up to the apps for meeting other mums as they usually have great advice pages too. And if you do attend any antenatal classes, make sure there's a group chat set up afterwards; don't underestimate the difference having someone at the end of a text at 3 a.m. can make. Twins Trust run a closed single-parent Facebook group and have leaflets that you might find useful.

Our strongest advice to single parents is not to neglect yourself. Stay as healthy, active and social as you can before and after the babies arrive. You need to look after yourself and you will need reserves of physical and emotional strength, particularly for the first few months. A freezer full of home-cooked meals and a mum buddy you can rely on for a chat and a walk around the block will keep you going. It will get easier, we promise.

***

Alison

My ex-partner has been supportive and my friends and parents have been extraordinary. I've been so moved by how kind people have been to me. I'm even touched by how the local shopkeepers treat you like a mini-celebrity!

Louise

The best housework advice I ever got was time yourself and do as much as possible in whatever time you have, even if it's just five minutes (forget quality, just clear it), and never leave a room without picking something up that needs to be moved somewhere else… Not that I do enough of that these days…

***

PAID HELP

We know that for most parents of twins, paying for

help in their first year is not an option. Only you know your situation and what would help you – and quite a few of our mums chose to have no help. If you are without the funds or desire to hire in a spare pair of hands, feel free to skip to the end of the chapter. A combination of routine, organisation and a big dose of 'going with the flow' can definitely get you through.

However, if you can afford it, paid help could make a big difference to your first weeks and months with the babies. It is worth saving and budgeting for, even instead of holidays, in that first year so you can spend a bit more time enjoying your babies and less time utterly exhausted. If you can only afford a little, then getting a cleaner in every month to do a really good clean of the house for a few hours could be a big help to keep you feeling on top of things.

For those who do have funds available, there are a number of options:

DOULAS

Doulas are like a cross between a birthing partner and a midwife, mostly for vaginal deliveries – and not that common for twin mums to have. They are often some-one who has had personal experience of birth and who has assisted at labours, births and in the early days of motherhood for many other mothers. They can be expensive (not available on the NHS), but they are on call for whenever your labour starts. Investigate how you could use your doula if you end up having a C-section, as she may be able to help in the early days with cooking, cleaning and caring for you and the babies, and may also help in establishing breastfeeding. There are also postnatal doulas who help specifically in the days after birth.

MATERNITY AND NIGHT NURSES

In the newborn stage there are maternity nurses and night nurses. They should have a maternity nurse qualification. Ask your local twin community for their recommendations as twin experience is really helpful. They are very expensive (e.g. £1,000+ per week in London for six days' care around the clock) but can help enormously in the first few weeks. They help with all aspects of the babies' care and will look after them at night, sleeping in their room (so you don't need an extra bedroom), bringing them in to you for a breast-feed at night unless you're bottle feeding or expressing. They will establish good sleep practices, helping the babies to know day from night and create a structure for the day. They will also ensure your health is looked after.

If this is what you want, you need to find candidates and interview them before the twins are born. By the time they leave, the aim is for you to be confident with your babies, so it's important that they help you but don't take over.

Night nurses are similar in qualifications but just do the nights. Again, it is important you interview them and lay out your expectations beforehand. If you want to set up a night-time routine, make sure they are not just 'babysitting' but are also trying to get the babies to self-settle and feed less at night – this is always the recommendation that Ella hears from nurses she works with and trains.

Depending on budget some people might opt to have help for a couple of nights a week over a few weeks rather than a full-time maternity nurse. This can make the money and budget last longer but will be harder the rest of the time. But knowing you have one night off a week can make the week go faster!

All maternity and night nurses should have an up-to-date paediatric first-aid certificate and DBS check (formerly known as CRB).

***

Georgina

I was on my own for five days after they were born and then the maternity nurse came, but then it became part of how we're dealing with things and with trying to get them to gain weight. They are a huge help and I wouldn't organise it any differently. Twenty-four hours a day – they get a three-hour break a day for five days a week. We're on our own at weekends because I wanted to be competent, I wanted to handle things and know I don't need them here all the time, and there's also the bonding thing. That's a bit of an issue – I'm not holding them twenty-four seven – thinking about attachment parenting I worry that that's not a good thing, but I'm actually there with the maternity nurse, I only miss one feed at dinner time and one feed in the night.

Katie

I had a maternity nurse for five days a week for four weeks and then it was Christmas time so my husband took another two weeks. During the day and in the night, to be honest, I found it essential – I didn't know one end of the baby from the other, how to change a nappy, how to bath them, I had no idea – yes, I went to NCT but they really dealt with the birth.

Alison

The maternity nurse I had at first was very experienced but she wasn't right. She was difficult to be around, she made me feel judged and undermined. When you're choosing your support, you're looking for experience with twins but also someone who will support you as much as the babies. Because I've since worked with two maternity nurses who are great I wish I'd had them from the start even though they are less experienced with twins.

***

NANNIES

Nannies are experienced childcare professionals who usually help during the day but may take on some extra hours and babysitting – they should have qualifications and newborn twin experience. As well as all aspects of childcare (and being experts in child development), they will do cooking, washing and light housework for the children but not laundry or cleaning for the adults in the house. With some negotiation you may be able to find some willing to take on some additional housework or cooking. All should have paediatric first aid and DBS checks.

MOTHER'S HELPS

Mother's helps are really an extra pair of hands for you in all aspects of looking after you, your children and your home – think about them as a cross between a cleaner, a nanny and an aunty. Again, find them through an agency or recommendation or online. They do not usually have nanny qualifications but can have years of experience and may be very knowledgeable and competent. They charge less than nannies but some want hours that work around their own childcare, for example school runs. They do housework as well as childcare usually and can potentially cook, clean and wash all the clothes in the house, not just the kids'. You can find mother's helps with twin experience.

People find childcarers through agencies, recommendations or online at Gumtree, Mumsnet, childcare.co.uk, and so on. Recommendations are likely to be the best – twin or other Facebook groups and forums can be helpful.

BABYSITTERS

It might seem daft to mention it at the newborn stage, but, if you don't have family or willing close friends living nearby, ask around locally for any great babysitters, or start sniffing round your friends' nannies or nursery workers. You may feel you are dying for a couple of hours out with your partner and with a little help you might be able to manage it in the first months, but it would be good for you to have some idea of who the babysitter might be before your brain gets mashed by sleep deprivation. (Have we mentioned the sleep deprivation yet?)

***

Ella

My personal experience was that the money I saved from stopping using outside childcare – a private nursery – for the older child two days a week, was better spent on physically getting help in the home and having an extra pair of hands, even if all three were at home more of the week. It took me a while to realise this but I wish I had figured it out beforehand, as it may have stopped me becoming as exhausted as I did and contributing to my postnatal depression. Having the extra pair of hands did however make the recovery quick, it made a massive difference at home and also gave me some special time with my son.

Louise

I used a redundancy payment to cover the costs of a mother's help for nearly the first year of the twins' life. She was mostly focused on looking after my eldest son and did housework as well. It was a big help and she was lovely to chat to and have around (my husband works very long hours and was travelling a lot in their first year) but, with hindsight, I could have had this person for a shorter time, and just had a cleaner in for the last six months. I also wished I'd made more time for my oldest son, just me and him.

***

Thoughts from a partner's perspective...

Hugh

Firstly: Be prepared! If you wait until the babies come before you start working out feeding regimes, how you are going to get your shopping etc., you have left it too late. You will be responsible for sorting out all the practicalities such as shopping, food, getting the mom and babies to appointments (remember: if she has had a Caesarean section she won't be able to drive) etc. Think through in advance how you will do all of this. If you are able to take annual leave on top of your paternity leave then do so. Your partner or the babies may have to spend a few days, or maybe even weeks, in hospital after the birth, and you don't want to have to go back to work just as the babies are coming home.

Secondly: Do not be afraid to ask for help. If people offer to cook you some food, walk the dog, do your shopping, fetch your post etc., grab it with both hands. Your partner will want you with her to help with breastfeeding, nappy changing etc. as well as providing emotional support and, especially if she has had a Caesarean section, help with her own washing, dressing and moving. So, expect to go a bit stir crazy and to be exhausted and take whatever help is offered.

***

Rob

Get help. Provide moral support. Be amazed by how your partner seems naturally good at it (and try not to worry if you feel you're not). Accept that your role is a very practical one. Stay as physically fit and well as possible. Remember it gets easier for everybody day by day even if it doesn't feel like it while you're going through it. Remind yourself to enjoy it for what it is as chances are it won't ever happen to you again.

***

SIBLING PREPARATION

Preparing older children who can understand what is

happening is very important; ask them to get involved with kitting out the nursery, and discuss how life will be for them when their siblings arrive: for example, where will the babies sleep? What happens if they cry? How will they be fed? What about if mummy is busy feeding and you need help to get a toy, what could we do then? And if you don't like the crying what could we do? Talk through scenarios and get them to have a guess about what else you could do – I think you will be surprised with how much they know.

For younger children, buying baby dolls and prams can be helpful, and there are lots of picture books about babies, although we've struggled to find any good ones that are easily available about twins arriving (although you could read books featuring twins along-side new baby books). It's also a good idea to have them spend time around mums and babies so they can see things like breast and bottle feeding and understand how small and fragile the babies will be. By a year, most toddlers understand (even if they don't obey) words such as 'gentle' and 'no'!

Think ahead about setting aside special time for your older child or children once the babies arrive, being realistic about what you can achieve with the help you have – it will be really beneficial for all of you. Your partner is likely to take the lead in this, especially if you are breastfeeding, but if you can spend even ten minutes three times a week with them, away from the babies, it will make you both happy and you will enjoy each other's company. Special time is a time when there are no interruptions and your child can take the lead in what they want to do – from a puzzle to a book to a game of football. Neither of us managed this particularly well, mostly because no one explained it like this and Ella certainly thought it had to be longer or more expensive or a big outing. But it doesn't; it is small amounts of quality time that appears to have the greatest impact. Louise went every week to a music class with her son only to find him acting up more and more each week – no wonder! It was the only time all week he had her to himself. It might be hard to find the time and get it right at first, but keep trying and your relationship and your children's future relationships will really benefit.

Remember to praise them when they are kind and thoughtful. Listen to their feelings and accept that they may be angry and jealous, act out or even regress a little. Recognise this as normal and give them labels for their emotions so they can talk about their feelings (reflective listening). There may not be any jealousy

– for Ella's son, his sisters are the best thing ever. For Louise's son, he loved them but was absolutely put out, sometimes a bit aggressive with them and would find sharing mummy at bedtime particularly upsetting.

***

Ella

I had a huge guilt about the impact of twins on my older son – I thought I would never have time with him and would ruin his life. We really, really beat ourselves up. I think this may be a difference for those who planned twins and for those who got a surprise. I know friends of mine with similar situations also felt guilty and worried for their older child. No matter how much we knew that Joey would adore his sisters – I think we wanted to protect our first child and struggled with this feeling of guilt.

A present from the older child to the new babies worked well for us (he gave them their rabbit comforters that they still use) and a present to him from his baby sisters was also cherished. Letting him open the door to new visitors and letting him bring people in to show them his new baby sisters made him feel responsible and was ever so sweet.

Jo

My son adjusted to the birth of his twin sisters much quicker than I anticipated. The whole thing was much less traumatic than I thought it might be. We had an early second birthday party for him with forty children a week before they were born because I was in a world of guilt. He was completely fine. I think things that we did that worked for us were that we didn't talk about the babies very much until right near the end, we definitely didn't do too much talking about helping mummy and this included being clear about what was emotionally appropriate with lots of well-meaning relatives. We did bring in a present from the babies, but he was pretty underwhelmed, and I don't think he needed presents that people brought him with the babies' [gifts]. We tried really hard to keep his routine really constant, he stayed in the same nursery so we didn't have too many transitions for him and I tried to make sure I still had time on my own with him every day. I introduced a new routine that he would play with the iPad as special time whilst I fed the girls and put them to bed. Not ideal but he felt like a big boy when this happened and he loved it (unsurprisingly!).

***

WHAT'S IT REALLY LIKE?

Preparing for the arrival of your twins is exciting and terrifying. Practically, the reality of the expense of two babies will hit you, it's significant. Emotionally, it will be hard to imagine how much your life will change, but expect it to. Line up as much practical and emotional help as you can, and that's probably better preparation than a laundered stack of carefully coordinated sleepsuits, as pleasing as that may be for the whole day they will last you.

When you see those faces for the first time all the months before will melt away and we hope you will know what an enormous achievement you have made bringing two lives into the world.

Chapter 3: Birth and Early Days

Your babies are nearly here! You are probably feeling utterly exhausted, incredibly uncomfortable but still very nervous about giving birth (unless perhaps you're having a planned C-section and have had one before). So, don't feel unusual if you're a massive (and we mean massive!) ball of anxiety. But remember that every day brings you closer to meeting these wonderful new people you have been creating. Hang on for a few tips…

EQUIPMENT TO ENTER THIS PERIOD WITH:

Bottle of champagne or other special treat

Herbal tea to keep you hydrated and dried fruit to raise your energy levels and get 'things' moving

Enormous, old (or cheap, new) knickers for postnatal recovery

Breastfeeding support contact details, for example local NHS or volunteer-run groups, telephone lines or private lactation consultants (if you want to breastfeed, do NOT feel any pressure from us)

Grim determination

THE BIRTH

It is worth remembering that a lot about the birth will be beyond your control. In some way, things won't go to plan. Your body will do what it can but often you have little choice over how and when your babies arrive; you and the medical team will do the best that you can for the three of you and nothing should be considered a 'failure', just part of your unique story.

In the labour ward or theatre room where you deliver, there can be a lot of staff. Everyone should introduce themselves but, depending on how quickly things happen, they may not have the opportunity and you probably wouldn't remember their names anyway. There will usually be two midwives at delivery, a paediatrician and an obstetrician (very nearby if not in the room) and, if you have an epidural, an anaesthetist. In addition, there could be medical students, student midwives and junior doctors (you will be asked to give permission for their attendance). For a C-section there can easily be ten or more people in the theatre, not counting you and your birth partner.

You will definitely be taken to theatre if you are having a C-section, but you might also go to theatre for a vaginal delivery if there is a concern about one of the babies or their position or if the obstetrician feels there is a good chance of you needing an instrumental delivery, which means a ventouse (a sort of suction cup) or forceps (a specially designed gripping tool) is used to pull one or more of the babies out. In the UK, babies born vaginally are usually delivered by midwives, with an obstetrician hovering outside on the labour ward in case there are any complications. A paediatrician is required if you deliver the babies before 37 weeks, or if you have an instrumental delivery or an emergency C-section, or if the obstetric team has any other concerns, which will be explained to you.

The NHS does not recommend the delivery of twins in a midwife-led unit, birthing centre, birthing pool or at home, no matter how well you and the babies are. There are significant risk factors at the time of delivery of twins that those environments are generally not equipped for. The doctors and midwives will want to continuously monitor your babies whilst you are in labour, which means you need to be close to the monitoring equipment (hence why a birthing pool is not possible for pain relief once you are in established labour).

But you can make the hospital environment feel a little more personal and homely by playing your favourite music, dimming the lights, wearing comfortable, familiar clothes and bringing along some items from home (e.g. your own pillow).

EPIDURALS AND PAIN RELIEF

In the UK, epidural or spinal anaesthesia (blocking your sensation of pain when you are awake) are used for the vast majority of C-sections but are also generally recommended for vaginal delivery of twins. General anaesthesia (when you are asleep) is extremely rare and will only be used for C-sections in specific circumstances or in an extreme emergency.

An epidural gives ongoing pain relief and is able to be adjusted – either topped up or eased off for the pushing stage and therefore recommended for vaginal deliveries, whereas a 'spinal' is a one-off injection most often used for C-sections as it is quick and easy to administer and doesn't need to be adjustable. Epidurals are recommended in the early stages of labour for vaginal deliveries because the effective and immediate anaesthesia they offer helps in a number of situations: 1) It could be a long labour (especially for a first pregnancy) which can be extremely exhausting; 2) delivering twins carries a risk of needing an instrumental delivery or emergency C-section, for example if one of your twins is distressed; and 3) the second twin may be in a position that doesn't allow for normal delivery so the obstetrician needs to turn the baby within the womb (which would be painful). Note that if you choose not to have an epidural and you end up needing an emergency C-section, the anaesthetist will usually administer a spinal anaesthetic. This is done in a very similar way to the epidural but can be undertaken, and will take effect, more quickly.

There is no denying that childbirth is a unique pain, albeit with the best outcome ever, and enduring it can feel like an incredible achievement. However, it can also be truly unbearable agony that lasts for hours and leaves you exhausted and the babies distressed. The epidural offers total pain relief (Louise has given birth with and without and can vouch for the difference it makes), and allows an exhausted mum an opportunity to relax, but it may also slow labour's progress. If this is your first labour, it can be very long, hard and shocking. Giving birth vaginally is absolutely possible but it would be sensible to prepare yourself for some form of medical intervention – with three of you to manage during the process, there are a lot of things that may benefit from medical help. Twin mums can be so exhausted and worried about their babies that a planned C-section is a really good option – and sometimes the *only* option, depending on the babies' positions and health issues. However you go about it, you get the babies at the end.

Pain relief – in particular epidurals – is commonly discussed in antenatal appointments so go along armed with any questions or concerns. For example, it is a common misconception that an epidural means no mobility and you have to lie on a bed, whereas in reality most hospitals offer epidurals which will allow you to keep limited feelings in your legs, enough to be able to move around during labour and enough sensation to feel contractions and the need to push when the time comes. The main thing to remember is that you have a choice about what forms of pain relief you can have, including whether to have an epidural early on in labour. You need to be informed of the options and given time to think about them. You can discuss with your midwife before delivery, in early labour or early on in your admission.

And don't forget that pain relief comes in other forms too – from back massage to breathing exercises, a TENS machine to pethidine, to gas and air. Whatever you go with, try to keep upright and mobile, change position often and empty your bladder regularly.

***

Louise

Having had a relatively straightforward labour and delivery with no pain relief for my first son, I felt very worried about the consultant's strong recommendation I have an epidural for the birth of George and Alice. Did it mean I would end up having a C-section anyway so I may as well plan one? Would I be able to push? What convinced me was an increasing feeling that I wanted to give birth 'the way I knew how'. In the event, the epidural was a relatively straightforward procedure, the midwives were very respectful of my reservations and I even asked for a top-up when I was about to deliver… the consultant politely refused my request as I needed to get on with pushing.

***

BIRTH PARTNERS

Your birth partner, the person you will have chosen to give you support during the birth, is unlikely to have experienced a twin birth before, and is quite possibly clueless about what to do. It's a good idea to go to an antenatal class together where your partner can learn how to assist your breathing and relaxation during labour. Don't underestimate the value of someone supportive and encouraging, someone giving *gentle* reminders to sit up and mobilise, keep hydrated and empty your bladder. Energy in the form of a favourite chocolate bar rarely inspires swearing in a birthing mother, although if she's vomiting through the pain, it might not be best timing.

More practically, it can be the partner's role to be an advocate and voice for you if you are tired and tearful. Some twin mums might want to ditch the birth plan, but it can be helpful for your partner to have it to hand, to know your preferences, be able to discuss the plan with the midwives and to remind you of it once labour begins (and understand if you change your mind).

As mentioned in the previous chapter, steroids will have been offered to you if your babies are scheduled to be delivered before 37 weeks. However, if you do go into early labour unexpectedly (see the previous chapter for more on this), it is crucial that you get steroids as soon as possible to give them more time to work. This is standard practice and will be offered, but giving your birth partner responsibility for making sure it happens gives you one less thing to worry about.

Louise's birth story

I agreed to be induced at 37 weeks but spent the week before doing all I could to avoid induction as I had stories of friends going into labour too quickly and all ending in painful instrumental births. I had three pretty painful cervical sweeps and, during my last, the midwife informed me I was already nearly 5 cm dilated so, instead of going home to eat more pineapple and drink raspberry leaf tea, I was sent to the maternity ward for possible admittance.

After spending around five hours and still no traces of labour starting, the midwives decided my dilation was down to having given birth before (plus the weight of the babies) and was sent home to wait for the induction or labour to start, whichever arrived first.

Friday morning at 8 a.m. we turned up at the maternity ward and were checked in. I met the midwives and consultant who decided to break my waters first to see if that got things moving. After a big whoosh and a clean up we were told to wait. I spent an hour or so bouncing on a ball listening to my birth playlist (specially created for the day) and was happy and excited.

By this time it was midday, so we went off to lunch. By 1:30 p.m. I was labouring pretty hard (involuntary groaning, the works). Then so hard, in fact, that lunch came back up all over the delivery suite floor at about 1:45 p.m. One of the staff members came in with lots of paper towels and handed them to Rob who then proceeded to clean the floor (they were meant for me). One piece of advice: try not to have a big lasagne just after your induction starts.

After an hour (maybe less) I decided to go for the epidural – I suddenly felt scared I was going to 'miss my chance' to get it placed in a moment of calm and didn't want anyone yanking around inside me without anaesthesia. A midwife checked whether I was sure a couple of times as she knew I wanted to hold off as long as I could and making the decision in the middle of a contraction isn't wise. I think the vomiting caught me by surprise so I was adamant this was what I wanted.

Having the epidural isn't particularly nice, and we had to stop halfway through for me to have a contraction. But I am fine with needles as long as I don't look at them. It's an odd feeling, it's uncomfortable going in, but it was honestly no worse than a lot of the uncomfortable procedures I'd been through to get me there (we had IVF). In hindsight, if I hadn't gone for the epidural then I think I might have given birth a few hours later if my last labour was anything to go by. However, I did have it and it meant for the first time in what felt like weeks I could lie down and really rest.

Unfortunately – and probably due to the resting – my labour slowed to a crawl. The last time I was in labour I carried on standing, moving, mooing like a cow and generally doing all the hip-swaying stuff I'd been taught at yoga for around five hours.

There I was 'stuck' at about 6/7 cm for the next four hours instead. Staff started to get worried and I burst into tears feeling so stupid and disappointed with myself – regretting alternately that I'd rejected a planned C-section and accepted an epidural. A midwife helped me to pull myself together and I got myself upright and resumed ball bouncing, hip circling and walking.

Still, I was given a syntocin drip, I think at about 6 p.m. This brings your labour 'on' and intensifies contractions although with an epidural already in place I couldn't feel them at all. Some antenatal classes make you feel like this is dealing with the devil. Don't worry – the team can vary and gradually increase the dose – as they did with me. I was given until 9 p.m. for them to see some good progress before the next evaluation.

At this stage I felt worried again. The lovely midwife who had been with me all day was going to end her shift. The brilliant consultant who had been so clear and understanding of my position was also clocking off. But the midwife handed over to another brilliant woman who really made the difference for the rest of the night.

I think by about 10:30 p.m. I was 9 cm dilated, so they told me I'd be going to theatre. Last time I gave birth I was squatting in a birthing pool in what looked like a dimly lit hotel suite in a birthing centre.

I was wheeled into the brightly lit theatre at about 11:30 p.m., and put on my back with my legs in stirrups. It felt medieval. I think the team were more nervous about this delivery than me.

I shut my eyes and started doing breathing exercises from a meditation CD I'd bought which really helped to calm and centre me on the task in hand. I knew Rob was there, that really helped too. All the staff started introducing themselves but I didn't want to know anyone's name, I wanted to shut out where I was, I just wanted to focus on the babies and what I needed to do next.

I searched out the lovely midwife's face and asked her to remind me how to push as it had taken me a long time to get the hang of it last time. I remembered the advice of my doula at my last birth which was to put your thumb in your mouth and blow – it works, try it now! – you can then feel where you need to push down (as it naturally pushes down when you do this). The midwife then gave me the best advice ever, which was to push like you are really constipated but don't 'let go' between pushes (the baby will ping back up). So I focused, I started pushing, and within about ten minutes George was born. Everyone looked pretty amazed and was congratulating me. They were shocked he had arrived so soon but I was focused and I think my body tapped into my previous experience. I had a rest, a little, happy cry, then shut my eyes again and got on with number two. And just after midnight Alice arrived. It was a wonderful moment. I have no idea when the placentas arrived!

Whilst I wonder whether I would have had a shorter labour without the epidural in place, I also wonder whether I would have had quite so much strength to push so effectively without the rest it allowed me. I also found the midwives extraordinary in their support and advice. You're taught in various antenatal classes that 'your body can do this, your body will know what to do' and actually our bod-

ies can do it, but aren't really built for having and delivering two – but can accommodate them and do it with help.

***

Rob (Louise's husband)

The birth was amazing – I'll never forget it as long as I live. Long, drawn-out and life-affirming.

Jo

I feel really positive about the birth. I told them I was going to have a Caesarean, I had a Caesarean, and was very happy with the outcome. I'd had an emergency Caesarean previously at two in the morning so a nice controlled Caesarean at 2 p.m. was great. My recovery was much quicker second time and I had really good medical aftercare.

Alison

To be honest, I felt a bit traumatised by it. I felt very 'done to' with it. I tried to schedule it when the consultant I had been seeing was there, but she was on holiday. It was a very busy room, like Oxford Circus. My mum was with me and she didn't have a chair for a bit and she is seventy-two – it was all a bit overwhelming. Everyone made an effort to introduce themselves but it was stressful with people barking orders. I'm grateful that it went well. I had mixed feelings about having a C-section instead of a natural birth. I had to reframe my expectations to think 'I'm really lucky to be giving birth at this point. Anyway, I don't want an emergency section, I don't want to put my parents through that.' I found it incredibly moving when the boys arrived.

Eleanor

I had a long time to choose which way to go, and there was a part of me that felt I should try to do it naturally. My fear was that twin two had a much bigger head and my doctor did say that if the first one comes out naturally then the second one can get stuck. So I'm really happy with the way it went [C-section]. I knew they were taken momentarily to be looked at and then I held them almost straight away.

Rachel

I really wasn't too intent on giving birth naturally, I didn't actually care too much how it happened as long as they were OK. I was in hospital from 32 weeks and, when I was admitted, both babies were head down so a natural birth was still an option at that point, although my consultant advised against it so we decided on a C-section. My pregnancy was pretty complicated and by the end of it I was on hospital bedrest. I didn't have any energy or any strength so the C-section was good advice and a good decision. In the end, one of the babies turned round at the last minute and the other

*was breech, so they would have had to do a C-section any-
way, so I would not have had any choice in the matter. If I
never experience a natural birth that's not important in the
grand scheme of things.*

Hugh (Ella's husband)
*We had a planned Caesarean section and it was all remark-
ably calm and civilised. We went in on the appointed day,
changed into theatre clothes and chatted until it was our turn
to go into theatre. The section was quick and simple and
we felt in really good hands. My wife recovered very quickly
from the surgery with very little pain.*

***

THE BABIES ARE HERE!

You are in a state of love, exhaustion, joy, surprise,
denial (still!), fear and love again; you are full of overwhelming emotions.

This is very new to everyone – even to those of you
who have older children (OK, apart from those who
have had multiples before*) – and it is a joyous and
stressful time.

*Oh yes, remember it is more likely that you'll have
another set once you've had one, whether through

genetic predisposition, maternal age or further fertility treatment.

WHAT HAPPENS NEXT FROM THE HOSPITAL SIDE OF THINGS?

A couple of scenarios may happen from here on. Some babies will need to go to the neonatal unit (NNU), which usually incorporates a neonatal intensive care unit (NICU) and a special care baby unit (SCBU) for those babies requiring less support and monitoring. Some will stay with their parents (that'll be you) and go with you to the postnatal ward.

Prior to the birth, talk to your birth partner about what you want to do if your babies need the neonatal unit – do you want them to stay with you or go with the babies? Sometimes it is helpful to have two birth partners around for this reason, if you know it's a likely scenario.

It is hard to give a fixed idea of what will happen after the birth since all babies are different. Some small babies come out fighting and need very little help while other, bigger babies need more. Louise's eldest son weighed over 3 kg and was born full term, but had to spend a few days in the NICU due to breathing difficulties.

Scenario one: babies stay with you on labour ward and go with you to the postnatal ward

Whilst you are on the labour ward or the recovery room (after theatre), the babies will be dried and wrapped up and you will be able to hold them and have skin-to-skin contact. This is a role for parents; skin-to-skin helps with the babies' temperature regulation and it is lovely for bonding. It also helps to stimulate the suck reflex and helps with milk production. Partners love this bonding time too – take off your top and hold them close, you've got a baby each to cuddle!

If you wish to breastfeed, the midwives will suggest trying soon after birth – usually within the first hour. The babies will try to latch (easiest to try one at a time) and start to suck, which is a great feeling – even if feeding only lasts for a few minutes at first. Remember, you are all learning to feed at this stage even if you have breastfed before, so do ask for help.

Then the babies are sometimes put in the same cot and sometimes in two cots. They usually get dressed in a short-sleeved vest, a babygro or sleepsuit and can be swaddled. Depending on the heating in your hospital and their age, the hospital may also suggest they wear hats.

Some hospitals allow partners to stay overnight but

many do not and may have strict visiting hours (so make sure you know the policy before you're admitted). You are usually on an open bay rather than a single room, although you can sometimes pay for one if available. Your partner, if allowed to stay overnight, will usually get a chair to rest in and if you're fortunate enough to be in a side room there may be a bed for your partner and your own bathroom. Often hospitals will try to find you a side room as they know you are likely to stay in for a few days and the more help you can get from your partner staying in the better for everyone. It is worth asking (a lot) when a side room might become available (keep asking).

***

We would recommend setting a timer and feeding your babies three hours from the first feed after birth and not letting them go much longer than three hours without a feed from then on; they are usually small and a little early so it is important to get on top of the feeds and be proactively waking and feeding them. Small early babies can sleep a lot – they have been used to sleeping the majority of the time in the womb and so can sleep a lot in the outside world and not wake to feed. If you have older children, you may remember them being more alert and awake in the early days but your twins are smaller and will have been born at least three weeks before your due date on average, and so will be sleepier. A word of caution: they may be sleepy and become sleepier because they are dehydrated or have low blood sugar or are jaundiced – so get those feeds in and get as much help as possible to prevent this.

Ask the midwives, the nursery nurses and general nurses for help with feeding. There is usually a feeding team of specialist midwives around too in the week-days – ask for them to help you with latching as they can be very good. They are not usually around in the evenings, through the night or at weekends, which can be tough going if you are struggling. If you are allowed to choose when you have your C-section then seriously consider the beginning of the week, so you can get as much help as possible.

If you don't feel you're getting the right support whilst in the hospital, look up your breastfeeding support numbers – Twins Trust has a great team of breast-feeding peer supporters you can speak to on the phone and private breastfeeding consultants can also attend to you in hospital.

In the next chapter there will be more detail on the specifics of establishing breastfeeding.

***

Jo

The [hospital] *breastfeeding counsellor had no idea how to tandem breastfeed, but I had breastfed before so it wasn't so difficult to work out how to make it work with two babies. Just before I had the twins, I contacted my old NCT leader who also worked as a breastfeeding advisor and asked her if she would be willing to help me if I was struggling in the first few days. I really wanted to breastfeed the twins and felt that the really crucial time is those first few days; it helped me to know who I would turn to if it wasn't working by day three.*

Scenario two: babies go to the neonatal unit

At the time of writing, over 40 per cent of all twins and multiples need care in a neonatal unit. If one or more of the babies has a breathing difficulty, if they are very premature or if there was something worrying in the antenatal scans, the babies will have to go to the neonatal unit. A paediatrician, and sometimes a neonatal nurse, will be present to talk you through what will happen next and why. What is important to know is that the neonatal unit is run by highly skilled doctors and neonatal nurses, with very high levels of care. This is what they do all the time, so your babies are in very good hands (Ella talks from experience of working in many different units with wonderful consultants and nurses; Louise had experience of it when her older son was born). Once you are able, you can be wheeled round to see your babies, and there is an open-door visiting policy for parents (but not necessarily for other family visitors without permission) immediately after birth. If your babies need a lot of help at first, they are likely to be in NICU – the noisier room, which can seem very daunting to visit at first. There are lots of buttons and machines and buzzers and some of the babies in this room could be very small, weighing as little as 500 g and having been born as early as 23 weeks. It can be scary and upsetting. Most parents of twins do not have any need for this level of intensive care for their babies but a higher proportion of babies in the unit will be twins.

Alternatively, if the babies are breathing well but are small (below 2 kg, usually) or a few weeks early, they may need an incubator and help with feeding, but won't need to be rushed off immediately. In this situation you are likely to be able to hold them and see them before they are moved to the neonatal unit.

Reminder: keep asking questions! There is a lot

going on and health professionals are very happy to talk through things with you. Partners can play a great role here, especially as you will be exhausted, overwhelmed and possibly in pain yourself.

Neonatal unit procedures

Babies under 34 weeks are nearly always admitted to the neonatal unit – this will be soon after birth but will not necessarily be treated as an emergency. The amount of intervention will greatly depend on how early they are; the earlier they are the more help will be needed. Commonly, they will be quite small, will tire very easily and are likely to need some help with feeding/sucking. Also, they can get cold very quickly as they cannot control their temperature quite yet and sometimes can become jaundiced or have low blood sugar. The babies may sometimes need help with their breathing, varying from a little trickle of oxygen to a Continuous Positive Airway Pressure machine (CPAP) to a ventilator which will give the maximum support for their breathing. Sometimes an endotracheal tube may need to be inserted into a baby's windpipe so that surfactant (a substance that keeps the tiny air sacs in the lungs open) can be put directly into the lungs.

Usually the babies will be placed in an incubator

(often separate ones next to each other) and given a nasogastric feeding tube – a small tube placed in the mouth or nostril to deliver milk directly into the stomach. This could be your expressed breast milk or – if available at your hospital – donor breast milk, or formula, or a mixture. Their temperature and blood sugar levels are monitored – the latter by means of a small heel prick. You can come and see your babies, touch them and hold them with support from the nurses. You can also help to feed them via the nasogastric tube (it may be strange at first but you can see it as another way to love and care for your babies). There will be time for skin-to-skin contact with the babies, known as kangaroo care. There is evidence that skin-to-skin contact with an adult is good for all sorts of reasons, including helping with babies' temperature control and mum's milk production. It is also a lovely bonding experience for both parents, although time out of the incubators will be more limited for very premature babies. Skin-to-skin time will also be limited if they develop jaundice as they will need to be kept under ultraviolet lights (phototherapy). Heel prick blood tests will be done to monitor the jaundice's improvement.

Your involvement is greatly encouraged and when

the babies are strong enough, and if you wish to, the nurses will help you learn to breastfeed. They will call you in the night when your babies are due a breastfeed and, if your babies are not latching on to the nipple yet (most do not learn to suck efficiently before 34 or 35 weeks), then the nurses will be encouraging you to express every three hours during the day and at night. All of this will help stimulate and maintain your breast-milk production. There will be a private room in the unit with breast pumps for this purpose and if available they will sometimes let you have a pump by your bed-side. The milk will be given down the babies' feeding tubes and the nurses will show you how to do this. If the babies are being formula fed then you will also be encouraged to give them formula either by bottle or by tube if they are not sucking properly yet.

If the babies are not likely to stay in the unit for very long, you will have a bed in the postnatal ward so you can easily go back and forth to see them. If the babies are staying for a while, and you are ready to be dis-charged, you will be able to go home then come in and out of the hospital any time. When you are not in the neonatal unit, the nurses will provide all your babies' care. In between feeding and spending time with your babies, we recommend you try to rest and recuperate as this will be a lot harder to do once your babies come home.

Leaving the neonatal unit

Once the babies are able to control their temperature they will come out of the incubator and into a cot. Once they are also feeding well with good blood sugars, good weight gain and improving levels of jaundice, they should be able to leave the neonatal unit (they can continue to have UV treatment in a postnatal ward if necessary). Sometimes, although not commonly, one baby may be ready to leave the unit and/ or go home before the other. At this point, they can either come back to the postnatal ward to be with you or may go home with you directly if you have already been discharged and no further monitoring or treatment is required. Sometimes babies are discharged with a nasogastric tube and the community nurses support the parents with this, but it is more common for babies to be feeding independently before they go home. Depending on the babies' prematurity and whether or not there are other health concerns, you may be offered some follow-up care by the neonatal doctors.

VERY EARLY BABIES

23–27 weeks

If your babies are born this early, then they are likely to stay in for a good few weeks and you will probably have gone home and be coming to visit. They will need significant help with feeding and breathing, regular blood tests, ultrasounds of their heads (which is not painful or invasive) and eye and hearing tests, all of which will give the doctors an idea of how everything is going. Again, speak to the doctors and nurses as much as you can and ask lots of questions. Write things down (both your questions and their answers) as it is hard to remember everything.

Moving babies to other hospitals

If you have babies born before 27 weeks, they may need to be transferred to a different hospital that is designed to look after more premature babies. All the doctors and nurses are trained to look after babies from 23 weeks but the neonatal services have been divided up into different levels of care, so some hospitals will look after more premature babies more than others. Your babies will be transferred in a special ambulance to a specialist hospital called a tertiary neonatal unit.

A rare issue arises when there are not enough cots in one of the specialist hospitals, meaning one baby will need to be transferred in a special ambulance to another hospital. This is more common with higher-order multiples (triplets and more), but if you are unlucky enough to end up in this position you should argue very strongly for a singleton baby to be moved instead of one of your twins (other parents will be unhappy but should understand).

28–34 weeks

The health of babies born between 28 weeks and 34 weeks is quite varied. Some babies can be very little but are very feisty and, although they need the neonatal unit because they are small and cannot feed alone yet, they may not need much help other than feeding and temperature support. Other babies may be bigger and yet need more help with their breathing and feeding.

Your time in neonatal can be a bit up and down, with good days and less good ones; it is emotional for everyone involved so talk to the staff and family and the other parents in the unit. There will be a parents' room in the unit where you have the opportunity to talk to fellow parents, which can be enormously supportive. The unit will also have a psychologist or coun-sellor on hand, if you wish to speak to one. And keep asking about breastfeeding support if that's what you feel you need.

***

Georgina

In NICU there are some very, very small babies and a lot of equipment so it's pretty shocking but then, once you are in there, the people there are extremely kind, understanding and patient. I had gone up to NICU, the intensive care unit, at 30 weeks, as I wanted to be familiar with it but it was too emotional going inside. We were in special care for six weeks and hospital for eight weeks and I did find it amaz-ing and the whole experience really, really positive. It's so parent-oriented I was amazed at the extra care and atten-tion – you could be a total mess and a bit of an arse and asking too many questions and they put up with all of that.

After 34 weeks

How well the babies feed and regulate their tempera-ture and how big they are will be the determining fac-tors in whether they come to the baby unit after birth or stay on the postnatal ward with their parents. The babies will be closely monitored and, if they need more help, they can be moved to the baby unit at any time, after discussion, and a plan made between the parents and health professionals.

Establishing breastfeeding when babies are in NICU or special care

Georgina (twins born at 31 weeks)
Hand expressing was really important for me before I got on to the pump thing. I found these videos online and I hand expressed with help from my husband who was really amazing through the whole colostrum period – he was sleeping at the hospital and literally siphoning the colostrum from my breasts. Trying to do it yourself – it's literally impossible with no baby, and he was running up and down to the unit – he totally thought it was the most important thing in the world. I think expressing milk – not only for the health reasons – was my anchor, it was my only way of contributing to the situation and it kept me sane because if you spend twenty-four hours a day not doing anything…
At least I felt like I was contributing something.

***

Establishing breastfeeding whilst babies are in special care for any length of time is a difficult job, no two ways about it, but most of the mums we spoke to succeeded and it was an incredible job they all did. Some mums got on well with expressing, while for others it didn't work so well. The more relaxed, hydrated, well fed and focused on the babies you are the better (just looking at photos on your phone can make a big difference). You must eat well, though hospital meals are generally insufficient. Ask partners to bring solid energy-giving snacks that are easy to store and eat such as flapjacks, dried fruit and bananas. Keep drinking water as much as you can.

There are lots of online videos and support that can help you, especially with techniques for hand expressing, but the most important thing is to keep regularly stimulating your supply for whenever your babies are ready to suckle. Some babies, especially earlier babies, will find it hard to get the hang of breastfeeding so you may end up feeding them expressed milk for a long time even if their brother or sister is feeding well at the breast. Most of the mums we spoke to whose babies were in the special care units had formula given to their babies at one point or another. Please stay relaxed about this – the nurses will be monitoring how hydrated your babies are at all times, and if your milk is not sufficient just yet, well, that's to be expected and accepted. It won't stop you from increasing your supply at a later stage. This will be a fraught time and everyone will be doing all they can.

POSTNATAL CARE – RECOVERY AFTER A C-SECTION

The basic issue is you will find it hard to turn and sit up, which means looking after your babies at first requires a lot of help. The anaesthetic (epidural or spinal) will slowly wear off and you will be given regular pain medication (take it!) and be seen by the anaesthetist and have regular observations done (blood pressure, temperature, etc.). The health professionals will take a close look at your wound to ensure it looks healthy and not red, which could indicate an infection. Your catheter will be removed. By the next day they will suggest taking a shower or washing with some help to start to mobilise (with your lovely anti-embolism stockings on) and sitting up as much as you can, perhaps in the chair for a bit. The advantage of the hospital bed is the automatic up and down function and you will wish you could have the same at home. It is hard to sit up and you will usually have to turn onto your side and then sit up that way; your abdominal muscles can take a while to heal. Peppermint tea and something to get your bowels going, such as dried fruit or laxatives will help, as well as sitting up rather than lying flat. Sometimes you can get a lot of gas in your abdomen and also pain in your shoulder, which can be very painful – talk to your midwife or doctor.

Once home, your community midwife will remove your stitches on day five and also keep an eye on the wound/scar (unless they are dissolvable sutures, which don't need removing as they dissolve spontaneously in 2–4 weeks). It will take a few days before you feel up to getting back on your feet and moving around but the recovery is much better (nearly always) than you think or hear stories about. Remember, people who have had a good experience do not often talk; only those with bad experiences talk about it (they need to). The scar heals into something barely visible (bikini line) and if you have a C-section in the future then they nearly always use the same scar to operate through, so you do not end up with two scars.

After your C-section, you are advised not to drive for six weeks – if you feel well enough and would like to drive before this, you will need to speak to your car insurance company as they may allow this with your GP's agreement. You should not do exercise, especially sit-ups, for at least six weeks; some say twelve weeks. Midwives may also advise you not to have intercourse for six weeks (stranger things have happened). You will have a vaginal bleed (called lochia) for a few weeks after delivery and so you will need a good supply of sanitary towels (or maternity pads). Night-time maxi pads can be most comfortable at this stage.

***

Rachel

I was in three weeks before the birth then nine days after the birth – they probably would have let me out after seven days but I actually asked for a couple more days and they were fine with that. My consultant and the midwives were very respectful of the fact going home with two newborns is quite daunting. I really wanted to feel back on my feet when I got out.

***

POSTNATAL CARE – AFTER A VAGINAL BIRTH

Your recovery will depend on how long the pushing stage was or whether you have any tears that needed stitching. It may have all gone very smoothly and so you may feel energised afterwards and able to move around much more easily than when you were full of bump, but don't overdo it. If you are in pain or feel that things are not quite right down below, please ask and don't suffer in silence.

The thick night-time maxi pads we recommend for everyone to deal with their lochia can be a real help, both to absorb the bleeding and for extra padding. Some mums have a gel pack which can be chilled and placed next to your pad for extra soothing if you have suffered quite a lot through use of forceps, for example.

IMPORTANT POSTNATAL NOTES FOR ALL

Some hospitals put you in touch with the women's physiotherapist but many do not. It is worth remembering your pelvic floor exercises from day one, regardless of your delivery. These are of utmost importance but we all forget them. A good place to look is online at the Association of Chartered Physiotherapists in Women's Health as they have great information.

It is normal and natural that your body will look different to how it was before the babies for some time, possibly forever. For most women, their 'bump' is still pretty big for about six weeks – your uterus has been stretched to its maximum capacity – and you may be in elasticated waists for quite a few months yet but, honestly, there are more important things to worry about.

It's also quite common to 'miss' your bump for a bit, but you'll get over that one.

Lastly, it is essential that you seek help if you are having incontinence problems, a prolonged diastasis recti (abdominal separation) or pain on intercourse that is ongoing. These are all very under-recognised, serious issues and often undetected because women suffer in silence and think it is normal or feel embarrassed. There are dedicated women's physiotherapists who can help, so please ask your GP.

YOUR HOSPITAL STAY

How long you stay in hospital, as a general rule, depends on the babies and their feeding more than your recovery. You may feel ready to go home in six hours after a vaginal birth or in a couple of days (even less in some hospitals) after a C-section, but the likelihood is that your babies will not be ready. They can take a few days to establish feeding even if they do not need the baby unit or even if they are great sizes and born at nearly term. Feeding twins is hard work and it is much better to establish feeding properly before going home than to get readmitted at a later date because the babies are not gaining enough weight (especially if you have older children at home). Plan for five days in hospital, an average stay (but as long as your partner or another helper can bring you clean clothes, you don't need to pack for five days). Yes, if your babies are good weights and you have breastfed before and things are going well, it may only be two days but on the whole it is longer. If bottle feeding from the start, your babies still need a lot of attention to learn how to feed, to be winded and to suck efficiently and so you will still need to plan for a few nights in, but it is likely to be less than babies who are establishing breastfeeding. See the next chapter for lots of detail and help on feeding.

WHAT'S IT REALLY LIKE?

If you ask any twin mum what the first few days were like and she gives you a coherent reply, she's lying. For most of us, these days are an absolute blur. Whilst you'll never forget when you first laid eyes on your babies and then when you held them in your arms, the days afterwards are about surviving on less sleep than you thought imaginable. The key moments you may remember will be when and how your babies arrive – always a story, always a miracle – and when your milk comes in and you suddenly get rock hard, enormous boobs swiftly followed, or sometimes preceded, by a hormone-induced day of sobbing uncontrollably about everything.

We know you won't need any encouragement but do take pictures of your babies, lots of pictures. Make sure you have a picture and video of *you* holding both of them with that incredulous look on your face knowing what an extraordinary thing has just happened. It will help you to remember the times in between the boobs and bottles and nappies and crying and sleep deprivation when you just could not take your eyes off them whilst smiling like a loon. Crazy, precious days.

Chapter 4: Getting Started with Feeding

FEEDING IN THE EARLY DAYS

In this chapter dedicated to feeding, we will start with breastfeeding and move on to bottle feeding. Most of the mums we interviewed did attempt to breastfeed and a few successfully continued for many months. We hope their experience and our advice will help you if you wish to do so. Bottle feeding was a very happy option for many of our twin mums, however, so we have included some tips for those of you who will move on to bottle feeding or wish to start with it straight away.

BREASTFEEDING

For the first few days, you and your babies will be

learning to suckle for the first time. This is why breast-feeding is hard for twin mums. It's hard enough when there are two people learning (mother and baby), but with twins you have another learner in the mix. A lot of the mums we spoke to for this book who breastfed exclusively, or for a long time, had previously breastfed another child and/or had good guidance and support. So if you would like to try, then please read on.

Remember that at first you are producing a small amount of colostrum. This is fine, as the babies will have stored up a lot of nutrition from you to keep them going for the first few days. But it is important that you feed or express regularly as this will help your milk to 'come in', which is when your breasts have their first full load of milk – you will notice when this happens as your breasts will feel harder and lumpy and full and you will want to feed to relieve the pressure. In fact, a soothing, warm flannel in the shower placed on your breasts might even get your boobs spurting away of their own accord. Take any pain relief offered or ask for some if needed.

SO HOW DO YOU START BREASTFEEDING? THINGS THEY NEVER TEACH YOU

Here is Ella's method, tried and tested by Louise and

many others, which is yours to read, adapt, ignore or incorporate into other advice from friends or family so that feeding works for you.

ONE AT A TIME OR TWO?

Start with one baby at a time. Only once you and both babies are feeling confident with breastfeeding should you try feeding two together (known as 'tandem feeding'). By feeding one at a time, you will be able to concentrate on each baby's latch (how they are suckling at your breasts) which is key to establishing a good supply of milk.

ONE BREAST OR TWO?

Naturally, each breast will produce a slightly different amount of milk, so it is important for each baby to have a turn on each side so they get the same chance for the same amount of milk as well as stimulating both breasts equally. There are some mothers who advocate dedicating a breast to each baby – some for one day at a time, some all the time. But we recommend starting twin one on the right breast (for example), and then popping twin two onto the left breast. At the next feed, you swap the babies around, and so on. So, in twenty-four hours, the babies have half their feeds from one side and half from the other. This method seems to have worked for most of the mums we spoke with.

Keep track of which baby has had which breast by simply writing it down, or look for a baby app which accommodates twins. Ella's trick was to assign a hair-band to one twin on one side and switch it after the feed to remind her where to start with the same twin next time. Your breasts will need about an hour to refill after a feed and you and your nipples will need a rest.

THE STEP-BY-STEP GUIDE TO HOW TO DO IT

Getting ready

Your babies are likely to be very sleepy in the early days so it might be necessary to wake them up for feeds. You can do this by taking all their clothes off except the nappy, tickling their feet or changing their nappy. Once they're awake, someone can pass twin one to you and you can latch him or her on to the right breast, in the cross-cradle position (tummy to mummy, nipple to nose – see below). Position, position, position! Make sure you are sitting up comfortably. Bring the baby to you, do not lean down or across to the baby – this can cause back problems. Use pillows on your lap so that your baby is level with your breast. Use as many as you need to achieve the right height.

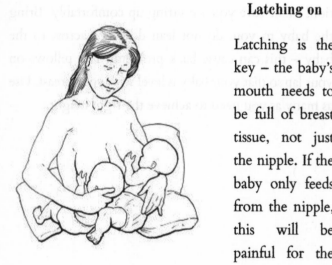

Latching on

Latching is the key – the baby's mouth needs to be full of breast tissue, not just the nipple. If the baby only feeds from the nipple, this will be painful for the whole feed and lead to sore nipples that can crack. It also means the breasts will not send the right feedback to the brain to produce the hormone to release more milk, leading to poor supply, which can in turn lead to endless snack feeds and endless wake-ups and a lot of effort to get back on track. If it is sore when the baby is latched on and remains sore, break the suction seal of the baby's mouth by gently inserting your little finger and then help the baby to re-latch properly. Don't just yank them off as this will be painful.

Remember, the baby can look like they are feeding when in fact they are falling asleep or comfort sucking. To be sure the baby is feeding properly, watch for the cheek muscles moving often as far as the ear, listen for a swallowing sound (best described as a soft 'cuh cuh' noise) and ensure they are awake (again, you can tickle their feet, change their nappy, whatever works). There are some good resources for you to help with latching: Best Beginnings has an excellent online resource called From Bump to Breastfeeding, and there are some useful online videos on many aspects of breastfeeding taken from Jack Newman's clinic in Canada at Breast Feeding Inc. (breastfeedinginc.ca).We also highly recommend Clare Byam-Cook's books and DVDs, including *Breastfeeding Without Tears* and *What to*

Expect When You're Breastfeeding... And What if You Can't? These are available to order online. Also try to get someone who has breastfed or is a certified counsellor to take a good look at a whole feed, beginning with the latching on – not just to come in halfway through and have a peek and go off again.

After a few feeds you may start to feel the sensation of 'let down', which is when your milk is triggered to flow from the breasts. For some women this is a warm tingling feeling, for others it can be a nearly painful prickle, but it can help you feel more confident, knowing your babies are getting milk inside them. It's difficult at first to detect this moment, and you will be very focused on getting the babies into the right position, so don't panic if you don't feel it at first.

Once the baby has latched on and you are happy that they are sucking, wait for their cue to finish – they will usually come off by themselves and can seem 'milk drunk' (slightly sleepy and content). They might 'pop off' accidentally before they are finished, but, if this is the case, they will tend to flail about a bit and keep opening their mouth and bobbing their head towards you so you get the message they want more. (Their tendency to headbutt any chest with anything resembling a breast when they are hungry can be very amusing. One of Louise's babies even attempted to latch on to her husband's hairy chest when he was enjoying some skin-to-skin contact in hospital.)

After the feed

Once you think they are finished, it's a good idea to wind the baby and wake them up a little, even changing their nappy to do so, then offer them a second chance at feeding (from the same side, not the other side). Once the baby is definitely finished, they can be winded and may need another nappy change if it's dirty (it's OK to leave a small amount of urine if using disposable nappies; cloth nappies will vary according to their absorbency) and can then be dressed, swaddled and settled down to sleep. If you have someone with you, they can do this while you start feeding twin two on the other side (and hopefully your helper has fully woken twin two while you were giving twin one their second chance at a feed).

It is feasible to do this solo, but, whilst still in the hospital, please buzz for help from the staff to get going at first. If you have had a C-section and have no one with you at hospital, you *must* ask for a midwife or student nurse to be with you at all times during these early feeds – you will need an extra pair of hands due to your reduced mobility.

In between feeds

The key to this tag-team approach is that while one baby is being fed, the other is being prepared for feeding, or settled after a feed. It may sound mechanical but it is not – all of this will be done with love and affection. But in these early days each feed can take up to forty minutes per baby, and needs to happen roughly every three hours. Sometimes, if the babies' blood sugars are low, the doctors may suggest feeding more frequently than this (it won't last forever, hang in there). So, if you try to get twin one fed, changed, winded and back to sleep before you wake twin two, you are even less likely to get any rest between feeds, which is essential for sufficient milk production. Some babies are very efficient and can feed properly in ten minutes, but this is usually after you've both been practising a while. It nearly always gets quicker as the days and weeks roll on.

A lot of mothers who go on to breastfeed exclusively, or who use very little formula, strongly advocate expressing in addition to three-hourly feeds as soon as you can manage it. The effect of this is to stimulate your supply and also to build up a store of expressed milk which can be used for top-ups or, eventually, to replace whole feeds. See the 'Expressing' section below for more information on how to do it and tips for success.

If you need some help getting started

The babies could be very sleepy or have difficulty latching and so not getting enough colostrum and then milk. This may have a knock-on effect on your supply and the babies' health as their blood sugar levels can drop and they are more likely to require treatment for jaundice.

Usually the midwives will be checking their blood sugars and their jaundice levels by taking blood from a little prick in the baby's heel. If they have any concerns, they will ask a paediatrician to review the babies and the results. Things that might be suggested include more frequent nursings, every two and a half hours for example, and/or more expressing after feeds, giving this expressed milk to the babies by cup, nasogastric tube, syringe or bottle. Their blood values will be re-checked to confirm if this has helped.

Top-ups

If your midwife is worried about the babies' weights, jaundice or blood sugar levels, top-ups of formula or expressed milk might be raised as a possible solution. Some hospitals may also have access to donated breast milk, often reserved for sick or premature babies. Whilst often essential for getting your babies' health on track, the problem with formula top-ups is that your breasts will not know they need to make more milk. Although it may be the right advice in the short term, if you want to exclusively breastfeed in the future, it is essential that you build up your supply through nursing and expressing as well. It can be very draining to be nursing, expressing and topping-up one baby and then the next baby every three hours, but hopefully it will only be a short, temporary solution (e.g. for forty-eight to seventy-two hours) to get the babies' health back on track. If using formula top-ups you could replace these with expressed milk once you have enough in store. Under the advice of the health professionals who are monitoring the babies and your health, there are two ways to reduce the top-ups. Firstly, it's important to be confident of the babies' latch. Then as the breastfeeding becomes more established you can either decrease the amount of formula by 5 ml each feed until you get to zero or you could move to giving top-ups at alternate feeds, then every three feeds and so on, until the top-ups are stopped completely.

***

Rachel

We did combination feeding because they were five weeks premature. One of them was a good feeder and one would fall asleep so she really needed topping up with a bottle. We were under quite a lot of pressure from the paediatrician to put on weight quickly as they had some catching up to do, so we topped them up with expressed milk (I used the big hospital pump) or some formula to make sure they were getting good quantities. At the hospital they got us into a routine with a small top-up at each feed. The girl who was a good feeder would occasionally have a breastfeed without a bottle but we did top-ups for the first six months.

***

If you are in hospital, try to come off the top-ups with supervision before being discharged. If this is not possible or practical for you, at least make sure you have a strong plan for coming off the top-ups at home, with clear instructions for detecting whether the feeding is going well (babies are settling between feeds, they are weeing and pooing at most feeds and their jaundice is showing signs of improvement and the community midwife is happy with their weights).

The number of parents who are still breastfeeding with top-ups at each feed for weeks after leaving hospital is high. Rachel did an amazing job and managed to keep breastfeeding but a situation such as she describes is very hard to sustain on your own – it's utterly exhausting and not convenient for anyone! All of this can lead mums to abandon breastfeeding altogether, earlier than they would have liked.

Some health professionals may be more comfortable with mixed feeding with multiples, possibly because they have no experience with exclusively breastfed multiples. Remember that the health professionals you see will vary in experience. Some will have breastfed, some won't; some will have helped numerous mothers to breastfeed, and some won't. Most will never have helped a twin mum breastfeed. Some will want the numbers and tests to be adequate without addressing the underlying issues. Hospital staff also see a lot of small multiples who are born early and need help, but most twins and twin mothers can breastfeed with support and time. Yes, you may need some extra milk from somewhere to get started or keep going, but this should be a temporary measure if you want to exclusively breastfeed. So, it is essential you advocate for yourself and your babies – ask for the right help and ensure you have a plan from the most experienced person you can find.

Ultimately, it is hard to give advice about breastfeeding twins if you have never done it, and certainly the best moral support will come from other mums who have breastfed their multiples. They are great resources of practical advice and moral 'you can do it!' support.

***

Hugh (Ella's husband)
On the first night one of the twins had slightly low blood sugar and needed to be fed with a nasogastric tube which was upsetting, but everything settled quickly and we were able to go home. However, having two babies to dress, carry, strap into car seats etc. took much longer than we'd anticipated. After a feed, we started the process of leaving the hospital but, by the time we actually left, they were due another feed. So, we had to find a secluded spot to park the car and breastfeed the girls before continuing the journey home!

***

BUILDING BREAST-MILK SUPPLY

Building up your supply is the most crucial thing in the first few days to four weeks; your supply is quite sensitive in these early weeks and needs to be enough for both babies. While breastfeeding, you need to consume 500 extra calories per child per day to support milk production. Eat nutritious food, drink lots of fluids, rest yourself as much as possible (you will have more milk even after a short nap) and keep trying to express if you are having to give the babies formula. Regularly stimulate supply by nursing, ensuring a good latch. Regular skin-to-skin contact also makes a big difference when you are feeding or resting together.

***

Louise

I struggled to establish my supply at first. One day one twin would lose weight, and the other would gain; the next day it would be reversed. And they were not gaining weight fast enough. A breastfeeding counsellor suggested that, after ensuring they had had as much as possible from each breast, to then swap them to the other breast. This is because I had one more productive breast and one more efficient twin. By swapping more than is usually recommended, it made sure both breasts were getting stimulated and both twins had a go at the more productive breast.

***

Food and herbs

Fenugreek is a medically proven herbal galactagogue (a substance which stimulates milk production) and you can buy it in some pharmacies and most health food shops either as a tea or as tablets. However, it doesn't work for everyone and it can cause tummy ache for some people at first. If it does work you should see an effect between twenty-four and seventy-two hours after first taking it. It can also make you and your babies smell of maple syrup, which is bizarre but not unpleasant.

There is a lot of discussion about whether the particular foods you eat have any effect on supply at all. Whilst not medically proven, lots of mums have said oats (e.g. porridge, flapjacks) are good for supply – they are certainly good foods for sustained energy. Although not related to supply, some mums have noticed certain foods make their babies fussy at the breast – usually foods that make you personally gassy (e.g. cabbage, onions) or that are very acidic (e.g.

orange juice) – which we think is worth being aware of at this early stage.

Health food shops often have herbal 'nursing teas' which contain a mix of herbs such as fenugreek, fennel (said to help milk 'let down') and chamomile (good for relaxation). The amount of each seed and herb is unlikely to have any effect on your supply (and is not medically proven) but the teas usually taste nice and will not be harmful.

EXPRESSING

To start this off, you might try to fit in two pumping sessions every twenty-four hours – once in the day and once at night, for example. You can express by hand (using an electric pump in the beginning can be a little sore). The nurses or midwives can show you how to do it, and there are great videos online (currently good ones on the Best Beginnings website).

At first you will only produce tiny amounts of colostrum (often referred to as liquid gold), which can be syringed into the babies' mouths. But between three and five days later you will start to produce milk which when expressed can be given in bottles as top-ups if needed or put in the freezer for up to three months and used at a later date. This expressed milk can be fed to the babies by someone else, giving you a chance to rest. The mothers we spoke to say that if they expressed in the beginning, their supply improved and they had enough milk for both babies. They could then stop expressing (unless they wanted some for bottles) once they knew their babies were gaining weight and settling well in between breastfeeds.

Hospitals have expressing rooms with really good electric pumps and milk fridges for storage. At home you can hire hospital-grade pumps (e.g. via the NCT website) on a monthly basis – they will arrive the next day. You can buy them, but they are extremely expensive, so try to look for second-hand pumps (and sterilise them). The more affordable models can also be good – look for online recommendations and reviews. A double pump will save time – most mothers like the Medela or Ameda Lactaline brands – and mums who have expressed for a prolonged period recommend expressing bras or halter-tops that hold the cups in place, making it a hands-free activity. Read up on how to use your chosen expresser beforehand, and if they have varied sizes of cups it may be worth experimenting to find the most comfortable. There are also non-electric manual breast pumps which are cheaper but none of the twin mums we spoke to used them.

The best time to express is after both babies have fed. Take a few minutes to eat and drink something and then express – maybe only for ten minutes each side (so twenty minutes with a single pump, ten minutes with a double); then you can rest and hopefully someone else can clean and sterilise the equipment for later. It is likely that the idea of expressing on top of all the feeding and changing you are already doing may seem utterly ludicrous. But give it a go. Even if you can only fit in one extra pump a day, your supply will benefit. Keep reminding yourself it won't be forever. You may find at first that you are producing very little, but the important thing is that you know you are completely emptying your breasts, which will trigger more production of milk.

Tips for getting more out of your pumping sessions: look at your babies if you can (even a photo will help), dim the lights, play some soft music and have a big drink of water or relaxing warming drink before you start.

TANDEM BREASTFEEDING

Feeding your babies together saves time and can also help a less efficient twin receive more milk (as the more effectively latched twin will trigger let down). Usually you can try this at home or in the hospital, perhaps on day four, once you are confident with each baby latching on well individually. If you wait until you get home to tandem feed, try to start whilst your partner or other helper is around. Once this is running smoothly, you may be able to finish the whole feeding process within an hour and get two hours off!

Most mothers we spoke to preferred to keep the babies on the same routine ('one up, both up'), made possible through tandem feeding. Consistency is key so if one wakes for feeding, you also wake the other for feeding – i.e. the feeding schedule is led by the hungrier baby. If one wakes from a nap, then you wake up the other one shortly after. This works very well for a great number of parents of twins and may be even easier with identical twins as they have similar body clocks, unlike non-identical babies. There will be more on routines in each chapter, adapted to the age of your babies.

Getting started

To start, you will need someone to help you get the babies properly latched (you will be able to do this solo after your first few successful tandem sessions). Sitting comfortably on a couch or bed, propped up by pillows, legs up on a stool if sitting on a sofa, the remote control, mobile phone, water and a snack to hand – here goes! Have your double breastfeeding pillow, or something similar, around you. Having been woken and cleaned, the first baby can be passed to you to latch on to one side, in the rugby position (body curled under your arm around to your back – see the picture below). Once latched, baby number two can be passed to you and latched on to the other side, also in the rugby position.

It is important to use gravity as an aid to feeding –

let your breasts fall into their natural position and the babies' bodies resting at the breast. The feeding pillows are slanted to help with this and you can prop another pillow underneath to ensure the babies are at the level of your nipples and you are not bending forwards or having to hold up your breasts or the babies. Now you are technically hands free!

Once the babies have finished, both will need to be winded one at a time (unfortunately there is no tandem winding technique!), possibly changed and popped back onto the same breast for a second try. Finally, both will need winding and dressing again (ensuring no poos in the nappy) and settled in their baskets or cot.

If on your own, you need to have everything prepared before latching them on. Have the babies on your bed or sofa either side of you, or in bouncers or baskets you can easily reach. You can reach out and pick up one baby under the arms and behind the head (a scooping technique) and pop them on the pillow and latch. Then scoop up the other baby (sounds very unfriendly but Ella can't find another word!) and latch. Another method of lifting is the 'cat-hold' – clutching a big bunch of their clothing to lift them – but this is not recommended for small babies because of their lack of head control. You can either wind them one at a time, as each one finishes, by placing them on your shoulder or rubbing their back, then pop them back on for their second chance; or wait until both have finished, place one next to you or in a bouncer whilst winding the other one and then switch. Then both babies get their second chance to feed.

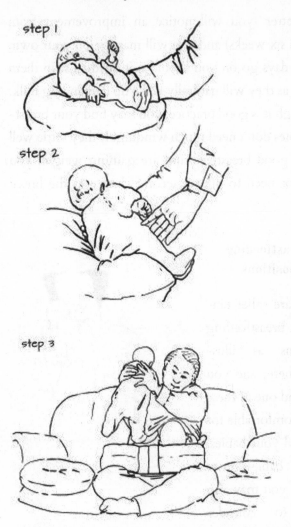

step 1

step 2

step 3

Tandem feeding will get much easier and quicker after
a few weeks – even more so once their head control

gets better (you will notice an improvement from around six weeks) and you will manage on your own. As the days go on you should not need to strip them to feed as they will naturally wake up demanding milk. Although it is good practice, you may find your breast-fed babies don't need much winding. If they settle well after a good breastfeed and are gaining weight, you may not need to offer a second chance at the breast either.

Breastfeeding positions

There are other tandem breastfeeding positions as illustrated here, and you may find one of these more comfortable for you and your babies. As the babies grow bigger, you may also need to consider other positions.

Louise

In hindsight, I started to tandem feed too soon but eventually it saved a lot of time and effort. I wish I'd focused a little longer on getting the latch right for each baby at the start, but

it worked out OK in the end (we had a few weeks of lots of expressing and swapping babies from breast to breast as their weight dropped outside of the comfort zone). I'll confess to feeling like a 'sow' on some days, but by the end I was proud of this cool skill I'd mastered. When they were both feeding well together and were big enough for me to kind of welly them around to get them into the right position on the pillow, I positively enjoyed it.

***

The decision not to tandem feed

Some mothers never tandem feed, preferring not to have both babies up at the same time, with the potential for both crying and simultaneously needing comforting or changing. Initially, this will take a lot longer but mums may find it necessary because one of their twins needs more attention and help to feed, or they may find it preferable for the individual bonding time it allows.

Babies' routines can be offset, for example, by half an hour – feeding one and settling them and then feeding the other baby. As the process of feeding becomes quicker and easier, the time taken will decrease.

BREASTFEEDING COMPLICATIONS

Feeding is work, it is lovely, it is satisfying, it is exhausting, it takes time to learn and it can also have some complications.

A massive topic in itself, breastfeeding complications are not unique to twins, and information is available in good breastfeeding books and online resources as mentioned in the previous chapter. If you intend to breastfeed, it is important that you know about possible complications such as mastitis, thrush, cracked nipples and blocked ducts. Being well-informed makes you more likely to understand if something does not feel right and seek help. An informed mother is better than one who is led to believe everything about breast-feeding is easy and natural – you don't just pop them on and hey presto! Lots of successful breastfeeders have overcome issues such as these.

Cracked nipples

It's not unusual to feel uncomfortable in the early days, especially when the babies first latch on – breastfeeding can take a little getting used to. Lots of mums use lanolin cream to soothe their nipples in the early days, and breast milk left to dry on nipples will help any very small cracks that may happen as you work to improve the latch. However, if nursing becomes painful, seek professional help – midwives, qualified lactation consultants or breastfeeding peer supporters will all be happy to help. Some mums who found nursing painful used silicon nipple protectors or expressed as an interim measure whilst cracks were healing.

Blocked ducts

Blocked ducts are also common – you may find a small lump that feels a little warm and tender where milk has become obstructed. Keep nursing, use heat and gentle massage before each feed and it can also be helpful to massage your breasts in the shower with a soapy wide-toothed comb, working from the edges of your breast towards the nipples over the affected area.

Thrush

Pain after feeds, such as a shooting pain through to your back or even down your arm, can be a sign of ductal thrush and may require medication for both the babies and the mother.

Mastitis

A sudden increase in breast tenderness and warmth with pain and fever could indicate the start of mastitis. This requires medical attention and, potentially, antibiotics. Websites such as Kellymom, the Breast-feeding Network and NHS have useful information for all these issues.

Tongue tie

Another problem it's worth being aware of is tongue tie – when the way the baby's tongue is attached to the floor of the mouth sometimes causes an inability to latch in the correct position and suck effectively. This can adversely affect feeding and supply; every professional who looks after breastfeeding mothers should assess for this, and there is treatment available. It is important to note that some babies with tongue tie will feed without any problems and some corrective procedures will not resolve the feeding issue.

Being informed about breastfeeding issues and being realistic about potential problems leads mothers to breastfeed more happily and for longer. Don't be scared – none of this may happen to you – but similarly don't be afraid to ask for help. None of these issues mean you need to stop feeding. It is also important to note that some issues can be caused or made worse by a poor latch, so get a breastfeeding expert to check your babies' positioning and latch to prevent further complications.

***

Ella

I had ductal thrush and it was incredibly painful, but no one had told me what it was and I thought it was normal. My GP did not know anything about it so it was not until I looked up Jack Newman's breastfeeding articles online and read The Breastfeeding Network's articles on thrush that I realised this is what I had. Getting the GP to agree to treat-

ment for this was a whole different ballgame, but at least I went in armed with information.

***

COMBINATION FEEDING (BREAST AND BOTTLE)

Some women decide to give some breastfeeds and some formula bottle feeds, which is referred to as combination or mixed feeding. If this has not been due to a supply issue this is usually to give the mother a rest. If your plan is still to mostly breastfeed, then it is recommended to start mixed feeding only once your milk supply is well established and feeding is going well – usually by about four weeks. This allows you to gradually replace one or two breastfeeds a day with a bottle of formula and still be able to breastfeed for months to come. It is important to note that for some women we spoke to, introducing any formula seemed to adversely affect their supply and length of time they breastfed for. However, for most it allowed them to breastfeed for longer. You could also alternate which baby is breastfed and which baby is bottle fed (with expressed milk or formula) – that can work well.

Some women feel that they need permission to give a bottle of formula – so here is your permission. Giving one or two formula feeds a day gives you a break, and is better than battling to exclusively breastfeed and potentially giving up because of exhaustion and depression.

If you are exhausted and getting quite down, then this can affect your breast-milk supply and you may stop much earlier than you wanted to – properly managed, mixed feeding may allow you to breastfeed for longer.

***

Rachel

Much like the birth, I think I probably deliberately set my [feeding] expectations relatively low. I would breastfeed if possible but didn't rule out the chance that they needed to be bottle fed. Everything you read is so pro-breastfeeding, making formula feeding feel like poisoning your child! Once they were weaned, I did bottles during the day and breastfed them morning and night. By the time they were sleeping through I would just breastfeed in the morning.

Whilst I remained open-minded, I did have moments of disappointment that giving them bottles was not good enough. But in hindsight, I don't regret it – there's only so much you can do.

Louise

After an initial struggle I exclusively breastfed my eldest son, Thomas, for seven months, and I really hoped to do the same for George and Alice. I really struggled to get my supply up for two and spent the first six weeks of their lives lying down, feeding, eating or pumping, with midwives visiting most days for the first month as the babies had lost 14 per cent of their birth weight. They got their weight up using syringed top-ups of expressed milk on top of two-hourly breastfeeds. I was told to fit three more pumping sessions into each day for forty-eight hours, but finding time to pump was impossible. When the babies were eight weeks old, Thomas was admitted to hospital so I found myself tandem feeding, still every two hours, on a hospital bed next to a very poorly three-year-old. That night I gave my first formula top-ups to George and Alice, and about a month later I started to give them a bottle of formula at bath time, which was the most difficult time of the day – and it really helped all of us. I am proud of myself for working so hard for them, but feel a little bit foolish for 'holding out' until such a crisis point.

***

Note: One mother we spoke to breastfed one baby and bottle fed the other one. This was emotionally fraught for her but was a decision based on medical advice and her babies' needs. It's a rare scenario but a possibility we thought worth mentioning.

NIPPLE CONFUSION

There is a big debate about nipple confusion – meaning a baby who is breastfeeding should avoid being given a bottle teat or dummy in case they find it easier than the breast, and then do not latch onto the nipple properly afterwards. Many, many babies in the special care baby unit get a bottle teat, a breastfeed and sometimes a dummy (to encourage non-nutritive sucking so they are learning to suck if premature) and do not show signs of nipple confusion ever. Some mothers report that it definitely affected their breastfeeding in a negative way and Louise happily used a syringe for all of her top-ups in the early weeks. None of Ella's babies had a problem, but her first son completely refused a bottle when he was five months because he had been exclusively breastfed and she had not introduced a regular bottle by four weeks (a whole different chapter in itself!). If you are concerned about it, consider feeding babies with a syringe or cup, or look for teats that closely mimic the breast.

BOTTLE FEEDING

If you decide to bottle feed exclusively, brace yourself for a bit of breast discomfort in the first few days as milk production naturally kicks in. After a few days, your breasts may feel hard and fit to bursting, but do not express milk unless you really feel you have to as this will stimulate more milk production and prolong your discomfort.

A supportive bra (not binding, which can cause mastitis and blocked ducts which can be very painful) and some ibuprofen will help. Use cool compresses such as a bag of frozen peas, or cold cabbage leaves in your bra, and stand away from warm showers. It should take around seven to ten days for your body to stop producing milk entirely.

PREPARING BOTTLES AND FORMULA

At the beginning there will be around eight feeds a day, so it is helpful to have lots of bottles to ensure you always have two sterilised bottles available to make up a fresh feed. You may want to try a couple of different types of bottle and formula before you feel settled with your choice, but, in reality, there is very little difference between the different options. If you feel there are persistent issues around feeding, speak to your midwife or GP rather than spending money on several different types.

Tins of powdered formula are much cheaper to buy than the pre-prepared cartons, although the small cartons are very convenient for feeds when out and about (and some mums used these at night). Formula dispensers which contain multiple pre-measured amounts of powder are very useful. The amount of formula you need for each feed depends on the babies' weight, so follow the instructions on the tin or carton unless given specific guidance by a health professional.

Current guidance is to add the measured formula powder to water heated to at least seventy degrees C at each feed before being left to cool or being cooled under cold running water. As the temperature of the water needs to be at least seventy degrees when the formula milk powder is added, do not let the kettle water cool down for too long after boiling it. A kettle with one litre of boiled water should cool for no more than thirty minutes and a kettle with 500 ml of boiled water should cool for no more than fifteen minutes. This method may differ from advice within other books and given by relatives and other twin mums but has been proven to eradicate any potentially harmful bacteria within the powder. An extra kettle can be handy (one for bottles, one for cups of tea), as can thermos flasks that will keep water hot for several hours in order to minimise the work at each feed. Given the guidance to add the formula powder to hot water, the easiest way to prepare fresh formula at each feed is to keep one large thermos of hot water (at least seventy degrees), and another of cooled boiled water. Add a small amount of hot water to the bottle, add the powder to the hot water and shake thoroughly until completely mixed and then top up the bottle with the cooled boiled water. Always check the temperature of the milk on your wrist before giving to the babies. Prep machines are also available which use the same method and are easy to use (but an extra expense). Bottle feeding does require more organisation than breastfeeding, but the obvious upside is that others can more easily assist with feeding your babies.

When bottle feeding, it is advised to start with one baby at a time and to wind during and after the feeds to ensure that each baby is feeding well and then being winded sufficiently. Whilst taking one at a time is partly about practical considerations, just as for breastfeeding, having one-to-one time with each baby will help you feel connected, happy and close at such a tender time for all of you. After a few days you are likely to start tandem bottle feeding which you can do sitting on the sofa with the babies either side of you, or cross-legged on the floor with the babies in bouncers, or on a couch or bed propped up with cushions or pillows. Some parents like to use feeding pillows. Lots of parents use their car seats to feed both when out and about. There are also a variety of bottle-feeding positions you can use to feed both babies at the same time, for which there are some great online videos.

Propping up your babies' bottles with towels, blankets or pillows so you can be hands-free is not recommended because it can cause choking, suffocation, ear infections and tooth decay. You may find that each baby feeds at a different rate with one finishing a lot quicker than the other. If you're on your own, the early finisher will need to wait for their sibling to finish before they are winded so we would recommend having a large bib or muslin handy in case one of them spits up any of the feed whilst waiting for their sibling.

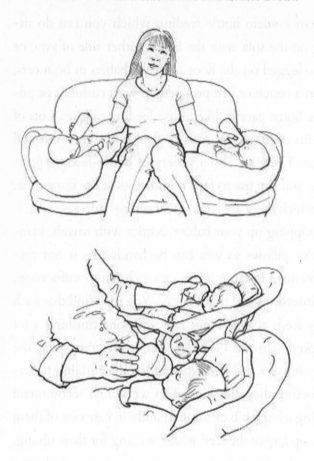

Sara

I was always going to bottle feed the twins and I was delighted with the advice I received from our maternity nurse. My top three tips would be: always warm the milk, burp after every ounce, and position the babies as upright as possible when feeding them.

***

IF YOU HAVE AN OLDER CHILD

Parents often ask how they can keep their older children entertained whilst feeding their twins, and it can be a very stressful time for the older children, knowing that their mother is not available to them.

If you are on your own and bottle feeding one after the other, or tandem breastfeeding, you technically have at least one hand free to read a story to an older child – but accept that this will be really difficult. Maybe you could retell a favourite story or sing some songs together instead. Many parents use the TV or an iPad as their treat when mummy is occupied with feeding. Don't feel guilty if you do this – it won't go on forever, and they will be delighted. However much you try to have other people around, or synchronise feeding with the older child's naptimes, it will never work all the time. Some parents we talked to had special boxes of cheap little toys, books and drawing materials that they could pull out as the 'box of treats' at feeding time, so it would be something for their older children to look forward to. This is something you can organise in the months leading up to the birth, or a nice job to give to your partner or grandparents.

Seeing their siblings for the first time will be very exciting for older children but the reality of a parent being unavailable to them and devoted to the new babies can be upsetting. Be prepared for the delight that you are back home, then potentially some crestfallen feelings as they don't get that much of you in the early days. Friends and grandparents should make an extra fuss of these older siblings and how special they are to be big brother or sister to two babies. Nearly all the older siblings we know of do become proud that they 'have twins'.

GETTING HELP

When breastfeeding, if you feel like all you are doing is feeding because the babies never appear satisfied and cannot ever settle – remember this can be a milk supply issue that can be quickly rectified with expert help. You can go to a baby breastfeeding support group in your area (ask the midwife or children's centre or health visitor or GP) or, if you can afford it, there are private breastfeeding counsellors that can come to your house to help you, as well as your community midwife. There are also good phone support lines run by the Breastfeeding Network and the Association of Breast-feeding Mothers. Twins Trust has breastfeeding supporters who are multiples mums who have breastfed their babies.

IF EVERYTHING IS GETTING TOO MUCH

If you get to a point of really not enjoying feeding and it is making you and maybe people around you worried and miserable – then you need to ask yourself if this is the right decision for your family. Can it work with a little temporary extra effort and the right support? Or shall I give myself permission to mixed feed or to stop breastfeeding altogether?

Try to lose those inevitable guilty feelings when it comes to your decision about feeding – everyone has a view and an experience but this is your body, your babies and your feeding practice and no one else's. And if the babies' weights become too difficult to manage, or they become dehydrated or jaundiced, they will need to be re-admitted to hospital where they will advise you to top-up with formula. Your partner, if you have one, will become increasingly worried about you and may be more objective than you in your tired and emotional state, so listen to them.

WHAT'S IT REALLY LIKE?

At first you need to take each day as it comes, especially

if your babies arrive early or there are any weight issues. Do what you can, listen to your midwives and doctors and don't panic. How you feed your babies long term when you are faced with the reality of what seem like endless, exhausting breastfeeds or endless, expensive bottles to clean and fill can have you doubt yourself and your decisions many times. Remember that you are a part of each of the decisions made about feeding, and above all else your babies need a happy, healthy mum who is able to care for them. So, if ignoring everything apart from feeding and breastfeeding works for you, or a bedtime bottle feed helps or if the immediate predictability of bottle feeding gives you the practical help that you need then do what enables you to give the best care for your babies.

Don't expect it to be easy – for most of us it isn't, especially those of us caring for babies for the first time. Feeding is your new job – with as much help from partners as their availability and your method permits – and it can be a difficult one to get to grips with. At some feeds you will feel like a sow or a bottle production factory line and, at others, you will hold your babies close, stare at their little faces suckling at your breasts or the bottle teats, and it will be the most wonderful feeling in the world, giving them the nutrients they need to grow.

Chapter 5: Early Days to Six Weeks

Let's kick off by saying that this period will be a blur, whether you and your babies are in hospital or at home. And it might not seem like it, but we feel compelled to remind you that things do get easier... much easier.

EQUIPMENT TO ENTER THIS PERIOD WITH:

Lots of clean, comfortable clothes for feeding and sleeping – pyjamas, vests and/or large t-shirts and nursing tops, jogging pants (and gigantic knickers are still the order of the day)

Sanitary towels (lochia discharge typically continues for four to six weeks after childbirth, at which point you won't need special maternity pads any more)

Pure lanolin cream or vegan alternative for your nipples (if breastfeeding)

Pad of paper and pen to note down what the babies are up to, questions to ask your health visitors and GP and, importantly, to list all the chores your visitors can do

Eye mask (cheap) to help you get to sleep during daylight

Tea: chamomile (to relax you), fennel or branded 'nursing' tea (whilst there doesn't appear to be any firm evidence on this, some mothers feel that it helped)

Box sets to watch whilst feeding (nothing too gruesome, you'll still be full of hormones)

Baby books (e.g. *Your Baby Week by Week* by Simone Cave and Dr. Caroline Fertleman) for more general information on babies

HELP AND VISITORS

At this stage, especially if you are on your own with the babies a lot for any reason, you *will* need help from friends, family, volunteers or paid help. Unless you're lucky enough to have something already lined up, now is the time to contact Homestart to see if there are volunteers available in your area – just a few hours a week to give you a break and help out around the home can be a lifeline.

You're getting to know your babies which is an exciting prospect, but you yourself will also be physically healing and your physical, mental and emotional resources may well be drained.

Like us, we hope you have found a twin buddy – other twin mums will be totally understanding of your tiredness, frustrations, amazement and stitches and know what an amazing and difficult job you will be doing. There are often new parent mornings for twin groups – worth a try for the emotional support from mums who have been there.

***

Eleanor

I look back and it was crazy. Especially because we had help in hospital and we were desperate to get out and get home. But it was a disaster – we got half an hour's sleep that first night. I remember calling my mum and saying, 'Don't go to work please come and help' in complete bewilderment and not knowing what to do with these two little things.

Louise

When George and Alice were about four weeks old, I can remember one morning Rob getting ready for work as I fed them both in the bed (for about the third time since midnight). He looked at me, utterly exhausted, and started laughing hysterically (more supportive than it sounds), 'This is ridiculous! You're going to die, look at you!' I feel fortu-nate we were still laughing about it however dark it sounds!

***

Twins are so exciting for so many families for so many reasons that you will likely be inundated with requests for visits. But remember the multiple mum mantra: a visitor is not a guest but a helper! Visitors can cook, clean, take the dog for a walk, pick up shopping, wash up, put the kettle on and do more cooking. They do not need to be waited on. People often want to help but don't know what to do, so help them out by instructing them. Try making a list of helpful tasks and putting it on the fridge, for example.

Watch out for some other pitfalls of 'helpful' visitors: if you have other children, visitors will often try to take them off your hands when what you really want is quality time with them. For example, once the babies are fed, ask visitors to take the babies for a walk so you can totally focus on the other child(ren), which is much needed for both of you (the parents we surveyed carried a lot of guilt about spending sufficient time with their twins' older siblings). Your older child will be thrilled to have some one-to-one time, and taking time to reconnect and explore how they are adapting can be mutually reassuring as well as a lovely bonding experience for both of you.

Some visitors (especially close relatives) can undermine your confidence by taking over or giving unwanted advice. But stand your ground; your partner can be helpful in sticking up for you too. In these very early days, emotions run high and you will be tired and overwhelmed as well as joyful; so, try not to let others get under your skin. Remember, if visitors are making more work for you or are making you feel unhappy, you don't have to invite them again.

***

Lucia

I had my husband at home for a month after they were born, he took parental leave then added a couple of weeks' holiday. Then my family came two by two to stay with us and help with the cooking and cleaning so I could really focus on the babies for the first month and that was really, really good. We were really straight from the beginning with everyone that came to stay that we needed help full stop – you're not going to be guests, you're going to be doing bits and pieces for us whilst we are with the babies, you need to help with everything else. My husband's dad is really good at cooking and he cooked loads of stuff and froze it all ready for when we would be alone with the babies.

***

MORE ON YOUR RECOVERY

Firstly, we'd like to remind you again about pelvic floor exercises so you can do them while reading this chapter.

After the midwife's initial onceover, your GP will see you at six weeks and check things are OK. They will check your blood pressure, that either your Caesarean scar or any vaginal repairs are healing nicely and will want to know if you are experiencing any discomfort – don't be embarrassed, mention if anything doesn't feel quite right to you. They may review medication that you needed during pregnancy and consider whether it is still necessary or your dose needs adjusting.

They will ask you about contraception and discuss what form you plan to use. When you do have sex (it might not be for a while), if there is any discomfort go back to your GP and talk about it. The same for any bladder or bowel issues including leaking and stress incontinence – you can get help.

Lastly, they will check your tummy for divarication, which is when your tummy muscles become separated in the middle. If the GP is concerned, they will refer you to a women's health physiotherapist.

Generally, be aware of your body – don't do anything your body is not ready for, such as heavy lifting or driving. The guidance is that after a Caesarean you should be avoiding these things for at least six weeks.

AN IMPORTANT NOTE: POSTNATAL DEPRESSION

Postnatal depression (PND) can come on in the first few weeks after the birth and is more common in multiple births. Most mothers have the 'baby blues' a few days after the birth, feeling sad and tearful. But if this crying persists, if you feel consistently unhappy, have unbearable anxiety over everything to do with the babies, are fearful of being alone with the babies or finding it hard to enjoy them, then this is not the blues, these are symptoms of postnatal depression. Other physical signs of PND include poor sleep or insomnia, poor appetite, loss of weight and loss of libido. Postnatal depression is treatable but it needs to be recognised and discussed, which is why we felt it important to include it here. Speak to your GP and health visitor; get help early so you can recover and get back to your old self, and enjoy your babies and the parenting journey. Partners can also get postnatal depression, which is very under-recognised, so watch out for this too.

Most importantly, having PND doesn't mean you are a bad parent, that you don't love your children or that your children will suffer any lasting emotional damage. It can be a biological hormonal response to pregnancy and birth and is treatable with a combination of medication and psychological and physical support.

***

Ella

The first three months were actually OK. The girls were born four weeks early and they did a lot of sleeping, from what I remember. Being identical they were similar in their patterns and breastfed without any problems. My son did not seem to remember being an only child and took to his role as big brother superbly (although I was very careful at remembering he was not so big really).

The difficulty is that this honeymoon stage does not last forever, the girls needed more attention as they developed, and rightly so. They also developed silent reflux which went undiagnosed for a while, and help soon started to disappear after the first few weeks. If I could have done things differently it would have been to organise proper help to start a few weeks into the journey, to help with the running of the household and to help with the twins, giving me proper time with my son and also giving me some well-needed rest.

The sleep deprivation I had led to a very low point in my life, and I was clinically diagnosed with severe postnatal depression. I was completely unable to make even the most basic decision without having a dozen other thoughts racing around my head about whether I had made the right decision, which made life with three children extremely difficult. Thankfully I received medications (high doses) and, when well enough to take the psychological support on board, weekly counselling sessions for a few months. The constant anxiety was all encompassing and unbearable, the worry took the longest to go away, mostly with medication and time. Gaining my confidence back as a parent, making my own decisions and trusting in my own parental instincts was a massive step, as I felt that it had been crushed. Thankfully I have worked through PND, and I got help with it early, and had a supportive husband, family and friends that helped me through this journey.

Thankfully the girls and my son are all healthy children, I cannot even begin to imagine what other families go through if they also have lots of hospital appointments as well. Help arrived in abundance while I was not so well and, as I recovered, I was able to take more control of life, my children and house.

But all this when I personally knew how to navigate the NHS and knew how things worked, being a paediatrician, married to a psychiatrist, of all things... I hope my honesty will help you to appreciate it can happen to anyone, and to seek help if it happens to you or your partner.

***

YOUR BABIES' HEALTH AND WEIGHT

Once the babies are back to birth weight (ideally by two to three weeks), it will be suggested that you go to the health clinic for their regular weigh-in. Ask your health visitor if someone can come to the house instead – you have two (and maybe more) children and you may have had a C-section, so this is a reasonable request that most health visitors will respect.

The babies will also have an appointment with the GP at six weeks, which may be combined with your appointment. The GP will review feeding and weight and examine the babies and check development is age-appropriate. Raise any issues you have, including babies being unsettled, not finishing feeds and crying during or after feeds which may include some vomiting – these can be signs of reflux or cows' milk protein allergy (CMPA), although health professionals and family may tell you these symptoms are normal or 'colic'.

***

Ella

Talking from my heart and experience, even if no one else thinks something is wrong, listen to your own maternal instincts as these are your babies. It took a fair amount of convincing and researching to get to the bottom of my girls' symptoms, even with my medical background and network.

***

REFLUX AND COWS' MILK PROTEIN ALLERGY (CMPA)

Reflux is when stomach acid moves up into the oesophagus, leading to symptoms of 'heartburn' and often accompanied by vomiting (but not always – this is known as 'silent' reflux). There are various signs of reflux which can include babies being unsettled, crying a lot at or after feeds, not finishing feeds, vomiting (or not) and being uncomfortable when flat on their backs but sleeping if upright in a bouncer. They may feed more at night and refuse feeds during the day, may be gassy and windy, may have explosive poos and/or may be very noisy breathers/sleepers. Few medical professionals have much training on this and even fewer are acquainted with reflux in twins – so don't hesitate to seek a second opinion from another GP or paediatrician.

Research is now showing that cows' milk protein allergy (reaction to the proteins that are found in standard formula and also in breast milk if the mum consumes dairy products) may be the underlying cause of reflux in many babies, and this is worth flagging up with your midwives and GP.

Reflux and cows' milk protein allergy are common and treatable – or, at least, the symptoms can be improved and made bearable – so do not struggle alone and let the babies suffer. The reason we emphasise this particular issue is that having twins makes this doubly hard. If you are armed with information you are more likely to get the right help.

FEEDING

Newborns should be fed regularly, roughly every three hours during the daytime. Remember, it is every three hours from the START of the feed (i.e. if you start the first feed at seven, the second one should start at ten). It is perfectly OK to wake the babies for feeding, and can be helpful during the day so that any longer stretches of sleep happen at night. At night, you can feed them before you go to bed and then, if their weights are good (if they have reached birth weight, are gaining consistent weight and the health visitor is happy), let them go four to five hours between feeds. When breastfeeding, a strict routine is hard to achieve in the first six weeks as you may need to feed more frequently than every three hours to boost their weights and your milk supply (more frequent feeding would be unusual in a formula-fed baby).

Feeding may take longer than you expect as they and you learn to feed and you may be learning to tandem feed (as well as learning everything else to do with your babies). You may find that, after feeding, burping, changing and settling them in their cots, you have only about an hour to yourself. So, don't put pressure on yourself to do anything other than rest and occasionally shower and change your pyjamas. Top tip: maintaining your laundry is an easy job to give someone else, such as a visitor. And don't be surprised if you don't feel like you are anywhere near a routine – hang in there, more structure and routine will be coming, even if the only routine you have every day is YOU having a cup of chamomile tea every evening; it will be a start.

Warning: there will be growth spurts. These occur at one to three weeks and six to eight weeks of age. During these times, your babies will want to feed more frequently for a few days in a row and sleep for shorter periods before settling back to their routine. Breast-feeding mothers often mistake this for poor milk supply, but the increase in feeds will stimulate your supply to match the demand, so go with their demands.

However, if babies are *never* settling between feeds remember to look out for the symptoms of reflux and CMPA as listed above, or for breastfeeders this may mean they are not latched properly or not getting enough milk. You might consider ways to boost your breast-milk supply, such as asking someone to assess the latch, trying fenugreek tablets, and increasing the number of breastfeeds or expressing between feeds to build supply or give top-ups as discussed in the previous chapter. For breastfeeding issues your options are local support groups (often run as drop-in 'cafés'), Twins Trust online and phone support, your local twins club, breastfeeding organisations such as the

Breastfeeding Network or a private lactation consultant.

***

Louise

*George and Alice's weight gain wasn't good for the first
six weeks, and I found myself breastfeeding every two
hours and lying down pretty much twenty-four seven in an
attempt to build supply (in between gulping down pints of
cold fennel tea). Looking back, it seems crazy what I was
trying to achieve in those early days, the babies looked so
scrawny, but then a month later the routine was pretty much
there and one of them was sleeping for longer stretches.*

Sara

*The biggest challenge was starting to sync into a [formula-
feeding] routine. They came home when they were four
days old and we had one night with them and then the next
day we had some help from a maternity nurse who was
running an agency with student midwives. She did a six-
hour tutorial with me which totally changed my thoughts;
instead of cradling horizontally to bottle feed them she
would hold them quite upright and then she showed me how
to wind after each ounce. I've literally never had any problem with either of them with wind and by six weeks old*

they were self-burping! She also recommended warming the [formula] milk and it was a very beneficial thing for them which helped with the winding and sleeping. To this day they are amazing sleepers.

***

A bottle-fed baby will have more of a routine and structure by the end of this period because you have a better idea of what has been taken in and what schedule to follow – again, roughly three to four hourly (formula takes longer to digest, creating a feeling of fullness for longer).

***

Emily

After four weeks I exclusively formula fed. At six weeks I put them on a feeding schedule of 7 a.m., 10 a.m., 1 p.m., 4 p.m., 7 p.m. stretching to 11 p.m., then the night feeds happened at 2 a.m. and 5 a.m.

***

On the plus side for breastfeeding, as well as the known physical benefits to babies and mothers, it will eventually become quicker and can be cheap (rental of pumps, a tube of lanolin and a couple of feeding bras still isn't a patch on the cost of formula) and convenient (no sterilising or preparation). It's not as easy to feed your babies in public as it is for singletons (I'm sure there is someone who has tandem fed in Starbucks but most of our mums couldn't face it). This will be a difficult time for a lot of breastfeeders, but, if this is what you want to do, keep going if you can, there is light at the end of the tunnel – honestly!

SLEEP AND ROUTINE

In general, up to six weeks of age, babies that have been fed and changed will need to sleep. They still need a huge amount of sleep, having been accustomed to it in the womb.

In the early weeks, feeding is the key to sleep and routine, so a good milk supply is crucial if you want your babies to settle and sleep regularly. You may decide a routine or structure is not for you; baby-led demand feeding can work very well in the very early weeks to build breast-milk supply. But whatever your preferred style, here are some indicative routines you can follow as rigidly or loosely as you choose.

Babies can sleep an average sixteen out of every twenty-four hours (in chunks of two to four hours), divided more or less equally between day and night sleep, interspersed by regular feeds. A full-term baby's sleep cycle is fifty to sixty minutes, lengthening to ninety minutes at three months of age and they will have multiple sleep cycles within a long sleep. It is useful to know about this because babies might stir a bit when ending one cycle and going into another, but should go back to sleep if left undisturbed.

Most of their awake time is spent on feeding and changing and little else.

Some parents find it helpful to start to follow routines such as those in *The Baby Whisperer* and *Contented Little Baby,* but we would advise that they may not make total sense for a good few weeks yet (and longer if your babies were born prematurely). For example, *The Baby Whisperer* routine is effective and simple but involves keeping your baby awake after a feed, which is not realistic at the very early stage as the babies can usually only manage to stay awake for a change and a cuddle before going back to sleep again. The *Contented Little Baby* books have lots of detail on how to structure your day, which for some parents was a very helpful benchmark but for others an overwhelming pressure.

Whatever routine you try to follow, the key thing is to feed regularly during the day to encourage them to sleep for slightly longer chunks of time at night and ensure they get sufficient sleep for their development and energy levels to feed.

Babies' ability to distinguish between day and night will generally start from about two weeks, and it should hopefully be well developed around six to eight weeks. Helping your babies to tell night from day (which they don't know to start with) is important. Some babies have day-night reversal, spending most of their time feeding in the night and sleeping during the day, which can make it difficult for you to get anything done outside of their routine, and for you and other family members to get sufficient rest. Babies may also sleep less deeply if most of their sleep is during the day. Some simple measures to help them are: 1) keep your babies' daytime sleeps to two to three hours then wake them up, 2) let them sleep in the daylight with a bit of background noise and 3) swaddle loosely (if you are swaddling at all).

Bedtime

Late afternoons and evenings (sometimes referred to as 'the witching hour') can be increasingly tough from about a few weeks old to three months. Babies can have a crying phase from being tired and hungry, and might cluster feed (feeding very frequently) and want to be held a lot. You may feel all you are doing in the evening is feeding and holding for a couple of hours or more. Try to go for a walk or get someone to come over and be with you or help – fresh air can help you relax as well as the babies. Have something to eat and drink for your energy, and de-stress by talking to someone.

From about six weeks, you could start a simple bedtime routine if you want to which will take a couple of weeks to accomplish. There is no rule about what this entails, but could include a bath (see section below) and a massage, even a story (with an older child and the babies in their bouncers), a feed and then bedtime around 7–8 p.m.(ish). It need not be too onerous or strict, but something whereby the babies start to understand that this means night sleep is approaching. It's also quite nice for you to have a point in the day where you know rest time is coming and you can go into autopilot with them. Adapt it to your personal circumstances and preferences – maybe put the babies to bed first to give you quality time with your older child(ren), or get help in from 4–7 p.m. if you can, so you can prepare dinner while the helper baths the babies or vice versa.

At this stage, they may start to settle in your bedroom and you may be happy to have a monitor and check on them every so often whilst being downstairs. This is a matter of individual choice, but some time alone or with your partner can help your sanity (although checking them every five minutes may not – so you may choose to have them settled in the same room as you downstairs).

Again, please use the twins support groups to ask for other people's routines, ways of doing things, how they manage and their tips – this is absolutely invaluable – they have been there and survived!

BATH TIME

Remember that babies do not need a bath every day. In the early days, top and tailing with warm water is enough – this means cleaning their faces, creases (under the neck, under the arms, behind the knees and in the groin area) and then gently patting them dry. It's also good practice to clean their eyes daily with cooled boiled water and cotton wool to stop them getting sticky. Keep the umbilical area clean and dry to prevent infection – the cord should drop off by itself between five and fifteen days after birth (if you see any redness or anything you're not happy with, speak to your health visitor) and then another week or so for the belly button to heal completely.

Once you are ready to start with the bath, in these early days we would advise bathing one at a time leaving their sibling in a bouncer in the same room or in someone else's arms and then swapping. As the weeks progress and your confidence and understanding of how to handle a slippery baby increases, bathing both at the same time using bath chairs can work well. It is crucial to have all the bath-time kit ready ahead of time: towels, sleepsuits and bouncers. If you are on your own, never leave a baby in the bath unaccompanied even in the bath chair.

Although it can work for some, don't stress yourself out about making time for baths at the end of every day if it's not manageable; you can do it in the morning every other day and that is fine too.

GETTING OUT AND ABOUT

Most of our mums found the first trip out of the house quite daunting, so make sure it is a brief one. Even just a stroll around the block to sit on a bench for a few minutes with or without the babies will make a difference. It is so important for your sanity – a small amount of exercise and a literal change in perspective will feel great. If you do not get out early on, even with help, you will most likely struggle to get out for a long time. The longer you leave it the harder it becomes, which can lead to isolation and feeling miserable – and can be a contributing factor to postnatal depression.

Your babies do not need to be wrapped up in cotton wool and can go outside. Babies at this early stage sleep a lot (so they can grow and develop), so why not outside in a pram or in two slings with you and a helper? As soon as you're physically able, try to get out for twenty minutes a day (whether just with the babies, with a partner or friend, or just on your own); the fresh air will benefit all of you. Babies love being outside in the fresh air, and they often sleep much better. For a short walk, all you need to remember is to feed and change them, snuggle them under some blankets or a light muslin, with a rain cover or sun shade depending on the weather, and they are ready for the outside world.

Make sure your changing bag is ready at all times. Refill it every night or every morning so you know you are always set to go. Two slings are excellent if you have a helper, and there are some double slings designed to carry two twins on the front (although

Ella couldn't find one that she felt comfortable with on her own). Try your local sling library and look at YouTube for a variety of methods and demos on 'tandem babywearing' – but do check with the sling manufacturer what the minimum age/weight of the baby should be, whether the sling can be used from newborn and what position the baby should be in.

If you have an older child or children, you will probably have to get out with them all on your own fairly soon for a nursery or school run, and all getting out together has its own challenges. Scooters and buggyboards can be great fun for older siblings, some mums sourced triple buggies at great expense, but many relied on their cars. (If you now need three car seats, make sure they fit across the back of your car.) Remember that one twin can go in a double buggy alongside a sibling and the other can go in a sling.

Even if the weather is not great and you can't get the buggy down the road, or you're too nervous to risk taking your premature babies outside, please consider leaving the twins with a helper so you can get out for a walk or a coffee on your own, with a partner or with a friend. This is feasible even if you are breastfeeding because, once the babies are fed, anyone can wind or change them and watch them until the next feed is due.

***

Rachel

I struggled to get out because we have two flights of stairs to get down with them so it wasn't easy. I first took them out when they were two weeks old but that was with help. Until they were seven weeks old, I have to admit I wasn't too keen on taking them out – it was March and cold and they were so small – I wasn't taking them out every day. But by the time they were seven or eight weeks old, I was trying to get out every day if possible – that wasn't easy, it attracts a lot of attention as well. The interest in my twins has calmed down now that they are toddlers, but at that time you couldn't get to the bakery and home without multiple people stopping you and when you get to the same questions for the fifth time…

Vic

I went out almost immediately as soon as I felt able to. I lived across the road from a park and my parents could get them ready and I would just push the pram out and I'd just have to stumble out. Just getting out, getting some fresh air, going to a coffee shop and having a coffee. I started with these tiny breaks every day then I'd take longer and longer walks, it was always very time-restricted because of the feeding regime; sometimes I'd just sit in a café, sometimes I'd meet my twin friend that I met at yoga.

***

WHAT'S IT REALLY LIKE?

This is one of the most demanding times for a twin mum. Your body will be healing and you may be struggling with feeding and establishing a routine at home or, for some, still in hospital. You will gaze in wonder at the two little people you have created and likely feel overwhelmed and exhausted. But later you will be amazed and proud at how you coped. Hang in there; just when you feel like you are reaching the end of your tether, the babies will start to smile.

Chapter 6: Six Weeks to Three Months

This is possibly the hardest part of your first year, and certainly the most incredible. You'll think you've established feeding and then a growth spurt will happen. You'll have a couple of days when you think you're in a routine and then one of them will stop wanting to nap. Parents will suffer from extreme sleep deprivation without the post-birth adrenaline high. Cross words will be spoken.

But then you see your babies' first smiles and hear them laugh and you start edging closer to a routine and start to feel like regular human beings again, and very fortunate ones at that.

***

Hugh (Ella's husband)

Don't take it personally when your partner gets ratty. Remember that they are tired and stressed. It will pass.

***

EQUIPMENT TO ENTER THIS PERIOD WITH:

Buggy, including sun/rain covers

Seasonally appropriate 'going out' outfits such as warm padded suits or vests and sunhats

Baby gym

Toys with mirrors

DEVELOPMENT

A big step here is smiling (real smiling and not just wind!), which usually occurs at about six weeks of age (corrected to any prematurity), and this is truly the most delightful moment you will ever have seen. Babies' vision is also improving and you will start to feel confident in their recognition of you and other family members. Babies during this period start to notice sudden prolonged sounds and may turn towards the noise. They love listening to you so talk to them about anything or sing – even if they can't see you, they can hear you and be reassured.

You will notice that they will start to move their heads more deliberately during this period, and by three months they should have full head control. Babies nowadays spend a lot of time on their backs (and they must sleep on their backs to reduce the risk of SIDS), which can increase the chance of them developing flat heads and being slower to roll or crawl. Regular supervised awake time on their tummies (also known as 'tummy time') will help to reduce these risks. At first, two to three times a day across your lap for a few minutes (not just after they've fed) will be enough; then, as they get used to that, you can place them on the floor, or on a mat with toys or interesting things to look at for longer periods. By three months old, a good aim is around twenty minutes of tummy time a day.

Make sure the babies spend some time on a mat or in a bouncer so they can get used to not being held all the time – this becomes impossible with twins as they get heavier – and gives them a chance to view the world from different positions.

Please remember there is a big range of development at this stage between any two babies and your twins are no exception. Also, always correct for any prematurity (your babies born at thirty-two weeks may not smile until they are over three months old rather than

at six weeks old, and that is nothing to worry about).
And try very hard not to compare your twins. Comparison is natural and helpful to spot if one of your
twins has serious delays but, more often than not, can
cause undue worries. Accept that your twins will do
things at different times – lots of the parents interviewed reported that twins take it in turns to be ahead
of one another in their milestones. Any real worries,
speak to your GP or health visitor.

***

Vic

*One of the great things about having twins is understanding
that every child has its own development arc. All my friends
with singletons seem to worry their babies should be doing
this and that, but you think, well this one's great at that, this
one can't do it, this one's got all its teeth, this one's still not
doing this – you don't stress about all the developmental
things as much.*

***

DOCTOR'S APPOINTMENTS

As mentioned in the previous chapter, at six weeks
the babies will have a check-up with the GP. This
involves both a physical examination and a develop-

mental review which includes, for example, looking at the babies' vision and checking that they are fixing their vision on an object and following it. Mothers will also need a six-week check-up, usually at the same time. There may not be another developmental check on the babies until two years of age so keep an eye on them, write down milestones and check them against each baby's Child Health Record (the 'Red Book').

Some babies will be under a paediatrician for their development and/or feeding, especially if they were born prematurely. Always write down your questions before you go in as it's quite common during appointments to forget what you want to mention – understandably you'll be tired and may be distracted by the babies.

Vaccinations happen at two, three and four months (actual age) and then again around twelve to thirteen months. You will need to book these as double appointments, one after the other. Overall, we have found the nurses administering these to be very helpful and sensitive but get ready for putting one crying twin back in the buggy just to trigger the other off. Louise managed to arrange a room at her doctor's surgery where she could feed her twins afterwards in order to soothe them.

FEEDING

The babies are usually now a lot quicker at feeding by breast or bottle by six weeks. We hope you have settled on how you want to feed – breast, bottle or mixed, babies together or separately – and have worked out a rough structure to the day and night feeds. It really minimises your work if a given feed can be only breast or bottle, rather than a combination of both.

The babies should be gaining a good amount of weight, and you can visit the baby clinic monthly for weighing if everything is going well (check their weight against the chart in the Red Book). If you are still feeling overwhelmed and struggling to get out, ask health visitors to come to your home to weigh the babies. The worst that can happen is they say no (but they will often oblige parents of twins).

Reflux and cows' milk protein allergy (CMPA)

Whilst reflux and cows' milk protein allergy were covered in the previous chapter, it is worth mentioning here that it may not be until six weeks that you notice this problem. If your babies are not settling after feeds, again our advice is to trust your instincts and get medical advice. Babies with reflux are helped by sitting up in a bouncy chair after feeds (the BabyBjörn bouncers are excellent for this).

BREASTFEEDING: ADDING IN A BOTTLE OR TWO

As mentioned in the early days chapter, if you would like your breastfed twins to take a bottle you ideally need to start giving a regular bottle of expressed milk or formula from around four weeks. If you are struggling to give them a full bottle feed, try giving it to them in a different position, a different room or from a different carer (who may be more relaxed). If your babies are struggling to accept formula, mixing breast milk with formula in the same bottle can help and is also a good solution for those with a small amount of expressed breast milk that is not enough for a full feed.

It's also worth remembering to check the teat size is compatible with their age (e.g. some teats go from newborn to one month). If you miss any breastfeeds – particularly at night – you may feel a bit full but it will settle down and you can express a little to relieve your discomfort.

Teatime

By three months, many breastfeeding mums decide to give their babies their first bottle. A common time for this is in the late afternoon when the babies want to cluster feed just as your milk supply is at its lowest and all three of you are at your rattiest. A 6 p.m. bottle can satisfy their needs while giving you a change of pace before the night ahead and a little more space to attend to older children (feeding, bathing or reading them a story).

Night time

You or your partner can give a bottle feed at night before going to bed, using either formula or expressed milk. This often works well as it means you can express at that time (if you want to, in order to maintain supply and have milk ready for the next night) and go to bed earlier.

Out and about

Many mums choose to bottle feed when out and about as breastfeeding two (particularly in tandem) can be difficult, although some mums find feeding one at a time perfectly doable. Bottle feeding can be in tandem in car seats or their buggy or you could let them take turns, one having a breastfeed, one having a bottle.

SLEEP AND ROUTINE

Assuming feeding is established at this time (whether

breast, bottle or mixed), your next priority will be sleep and routine. A routine can be as military or as laid back as suits your family. But having a basic structure to the day and night can help both the babies and you to understand each other and stay calm. And after the hand-to-mouth struggle of the first six weeks, you will be looking forward to any glimmers of life beyond a functional existence for yourselves.

Again, we personally advise you establish a routine whereby both babies do the same thing at the same time – this can really help you plan your day and get some rest. Ella and Louise both found feeding the babies at the same time – a 'one up, both up' routine – invaluable. This is especially important at night so you are not offering a never-ending milk buffet and can maximise your sleep – sleep which enables you to care for them more effectively. In the daytime, Ella always put them both down at the same time for their naps and if one woke up from their nap, the other had a twenty-minute grace period before being woken up too!

Some mums, however, do prefer to feed their twins separately, finding it easier to manage one at a time and enjoying one-to-one time with each baby. This is your choice but it may mean less sleep and rest time for you. There are also mums who have two very different twins in terms of size and feeding pattern.

Please seek or accept help at this time whenever you can – it is an utterly exhausting period, and any nappy changed or bottle prepared will be a help.

***

Jibecke

We had a routine from the beginning – possibly too much in the first weeks – but after that it was very helpful. But it's good to remember if you break it, it's no big deal. We would rigidly wake them up every three hours – that meant we sometimes had to blow in their faces to keep them awake so they would eat. If one woke up in the night, the other one was going to be woken up.

Katie

After six weeks I had no help so I had to do all the feeds myself. With the two bouncy chairs (they slept in them), I would feed them with two bottles or I would breastfeed one and bottle feed the other in one. My husband works hard and travels a lot during the week so it was only me. A two-camera monitor was great because we had one downstairs and one in our bedroom. I could put the camera on them and go upstairs and have a shower.

Eleanor

Keep it as simple as you can with routines. Ours was four
feeds – not necessarily at exact times, say between ten and
eleven and between two and three – and you build your day
around that. Yes, you are living by your routine but it makes
it much more likely that you will succeed by sticking to it.

***

ESTABLISHING YOUR OWN ROUTINE

Your babies will start to 'wake up' more now; they are
more aware of their surroundings. They will still need
about sixteen hours sleep out of twenty-four. They
will often nap after feeds and changes; the rough core
naptimes are likely to be after breakfast, after lunch and
then after teatime. Babies generally need to sleep after
around two hours of being awake – look for the cues
such as rubbing eyes and yawning, and try not to let
them stay awake much longer than that as they will get
fractious.

Mums we spoke to found the most useful examples
of set routines came from books such as *Your Baby*
Week by Week by Simone Cave and Dr Caroline
Fertleman, *Your Baby Month by Month*, Gina Ford's *A*
Contented House with Twins or Tracy Hogg's *Secrets of*
The Baby Whisperer. Just remember that, as they grow,

they need more awake time and less sleep during the day – too much daytime sleep at this stage will impact on the all-important night-time sleep and in establishing long daytime naps.

The 'Baby Whisperer', Tracy Hogg, talks about the 'EASY' routine – Eat, Awake, Sleep and You time. This is roughly what babies seem to do without you doing too much. The main point is that the babies should spend time awake after feeding – don't encourage them to associate the breast or bottle with going to sleep because you could be stuck feeding them every time you need them to sleep. Try to put the babies down to settle and sleep when they are semi-awake or drowsy, but not fully asleep in your arms or at the breast or bottle. This will set up good habits and was one of the best pieces of advice Ella followed.

That said, if feeding to sleep is the only way that works for your babies (like Louise's), do not worry just yet. If they are napping regularly, that is a major win in itself, and you can work on stopping the feed-to-sleep once you've got them into a schedule (Elizabeth Pantley's *No-Cry Sleep Solution* has some good steps to help you with that). Also, take them out in the buggy to nap as that will prove to you that they can go to sleep without your boob or the bottle in their mouth.

And remember that You time is your (important) responsibility. Sleep is probably your highest priority, but do whatever makes you feel human – a bath, listening to some music or an audio book, cleaning out the mouldy grouting in the bath (joke); just don't expect to be able to read anything more challenging than your Facebook feed for a few months yet.

***

Jo

They were pretty much feeding every three hours by about six weeks but we introduced a more formal three-hourly routine at that time when we realised they (and we) needed a bit more structure. The best book I read to help with routines was Baby Secrets *by Jo Tantum. I definitely don't feel like we forced anything on them, I think the routine just helped them know what to expect.*

The other thing that we used with our twins, but which we hadn't used with my son, was dummies. They took to them very easily, and because they had awful reflux and used to vomit a lot I couldn't always feed them to settle so dummies felt like the right thing.

Another tip I have is to get them used to sleeping somewhere other than their cot during the day. We always put ours to sleep in the buggy during the day – then we could take them out. It really helps if they can get used to sleeping in a light room as well, otherwise life can become even more restricted if you need to be at home in a dark room every few hours!

Rachel

I picked up the Gina Ford twins book when they were six weeks old and actually found that they were doing what she states as the ideal routine quite naturally anyway. We did vary from her routine in that we didn't do swaddling or wake them up, but we stuck to the feeding times and the naps seemed to fall in place. So, we were relatively strict without being too prescriptive.

***

DAYTIME NAPS

A simple tip is to introduce naps in the same way each time by always putting them into a baby sleeping bag or with the same blanket, using a phrase such as 'sleepy time' or 'naptime now', maybe with a light projector or song that plays every time you put them down – this will all start to get your babies used to napping and create cues for them to understand what happens next. We would also suggest getting one nap really regular before moving on to the others. So, if the babies seem to go down well in the morning, do the morning nap at the same time every day, with the same pattern of activities. Once it's going smoothly, it will give you the confidence to tackle the afternoon nap, and will give the babies some structured cues to help them with their other naptimes. The key to a routine is 'fake it till you make it' – pretend that it's working until it does. Persistence really pays off – but preserve your sanity by not trying to tackle every aspect of a routine at once.

Swaddling may have helped you along the way but it commonly stops by three months as babies will start to break free. A good substitute at this point is a baby sleeping bag, such as a Grobag, that keeps the baby warm and can't be kicked off or cover their face.

BEDTIME ROUTINE

Now is the time most parents try to start a little bed-time routine, including a bath, a quiet feed and then bed. This is not set in stone and can take a lot longer for some babies, especially when you have two to get ready. The previous chapter contains some tips for how to survive their first baths.

At six weeks, some parents may try a split feed around bath time: offering half a feed before the bath to take the edge off any hunger, and then finishing the

feed after the babies are in their nightclothes in a quiet
and dim room just before bed (maybe even reading
a little story between the feed and bed). Some babies
are so tired that they'll happily go down by 6:30 p.m.;
keeping them up past 7 p.m. can lead to chaos and
misery. Others may happily stay up later (whether you
will is another matter). Look for your babies' cues and
leads and trust your instincts – which you can be more
confident of day by day.

***

Emily

*At nine weeks I moved them to four-hour feeding schedules
and followed the 'bath bottle bed' routine every night reli-
giously from that time. I also used to nap them downstairs
during the day, put them in the cot upstairs after 7 p.m.,
using a blackout blind and Ewan the dream sheep* [a night
light]. *As mine were born at the appropriate weight, and
I had no major feeding issues, from the nine-week mark, I
gave them bigger feeds during the day and smaller feeds at
night so their overall daily allowance of milk was right for
the weight.*

***

NIGHT TIME

At six to eight weeks of age, most babies begin to sleep for shorter periods during the day and longer periods at night, though most continue to wake up to feed during the night. From around eight weeks, the babies really start to understand the difference between night and day, which is good news. Their sleep cycle will also be increasing from fifty to sixty minutes at term, to ninety minutes at around three months of age where it will remain for the rest of their life. By three months, their sleep patterns are maturing; this means they will rouse less often, sleeping for longer periods of seven to eight hours a night. Naturally, the first part of the routine you really want to conquer for your own sanity is night time.

After the bedtime feed some parents will wait for the babies to 'naturally' wake up for their night feeds. Others wake the babies up (if they haven't already) to feed them, perhaps around 10:30 p.m. (sometimes called the 'dream feed' because the babies often don't fully wake up for this one) and then pray for only one wake-up the other side of midnight. Either way, some overnight feeds will slowly be dropped, with the last one moving closer to 6 a.m. That said, some babies will still be awake for more feeds during the night – it's just how their metabolisms are working at the moment. Stay calm, it won't last forever and there will be more help in the next chapters.

SUDDEN INFANT DEATH SYNDROME (SIDS)

The riskiest time for SIDS, also called 'cot death', is three to six months, but it can happen anytime from newborn to nine months, although thankfully is now very rare. Remember, to reduce the risk of SIDS, babies must always be put to sleep on their backs and not their tummies. Babies should always sleep on a brand-new mattress – not a hand-me-down, and there needs to be no smoking near the babies or even in the house.

Babies should sleep in a room with a temperature of sixteen to twenty degrees, with appropriate clothing and blankets to prevent overheating. In summer, you may find your room gets hotter than twenty degrees during the night – don't panic, open the window and consider buying a fan. Some tips that may help with your room temperature is to ensure the room is kept shaded at all times, and to put a cold, damp towel up at the window to cool the incoming air.

To check the babies' body temperature, feel their

chests and backs; if they feel very warm, remove a layer of bedding or clothing – in high temperatures they can sleep just wearing their nappies. This is also where you should check if you're worried they are too cold – cool hands, feet and forehead are fine. It's the chest and back that will give you a real indication of whether the baby is too cold. In that case, add a layer of clothing or another blanket under their armpits tucked under the mattress (making sure it's a breathable cotton blanket such as those labelled 'cellular' i.e. hospital style, light cotton with holes).

Whilst the NHS advises that babies should be sleeping in the same room as their parents until six months, they advise against co-sleeping altogether. If you do co-sleep with your babies, whether by accident or intentionally, it must be done in the safest way possible – keep the babies away from duvets, sheets or pillows. Do not co-sleep if either you or your partner have been drinking alcohol or have taken any drug or medicine which may make you drowsy.

***

Sally

With my first daughter we decided that we would try to meet her needs before she cried, to try to keep her happy –

she was a very happy baby, very content and never cried! So, we fed on demand (bottle fed), which involved two-hourly feeds by the time she was four weeks old. We noticed that as her feeding increased during the day she wanted less at night. We mastered dream feeding early on and so at night, as soon as I heard her start to stir, I would give her a bottle in her sleep rather than waiting for her to wake up and cry for a feed. At five weeks we started using her dummy to prolong the 4 a.m. feed by thirty minutes each night, this involves having to be awake a few nights to keep an eye on her to make sure the dummy goes straight back in and be ready with a bottle. By six weeks she was going through from her dream feed at 9 p.m. to 7 a.m.

We repeated this with my second daughter – everyone had told us we were just lucky with our first and so we didn't expect it would work again. It did – we started delaying feeds at five weeks by thirty minutes, and again by six weeks she was sleeping through.

The triplets were born five weeks early and as such we started the night-feeding routine and stock-feeding daytime pattern from their due date. Their feeds naturally progressed to two-hourly feeds during the day and at five weeks old (corrected) I started delaying feeds with dummies during a half term. They slept through the night by the last day of the half term.

The important things for me in doing this are the following, and obviously just my opinion:

I believe that if a baby cries it needs something – by meeting their needs during the day you are getting to know your own baby, rather than trying to apply a routine written by someone else which can often not fit with your own babies' needs. As such, we tried to pre-empt their needs in the early days, which led us to establish a routine very early on that the baby set with our guidance – we didn't have three routines for the triplets yet they all settled into the same pattern. A happy baby is by far easier than an unhappy baby!

Dummies were a must for us; they were given to the triplets in SCBU and helped us prolong the feeds. I am unsure this can be done with breastfeeding – I can't comment as I never breastfed.

You need to set a date that you want your baby to sleep through by, they need to be big enough by this stage and, more importantly, taking their quota of milk during the day.

You need to prolong the feed by an amount of time every night – this involves a week of being alert around the time the baby was naturally waking up – which is why we went *with a half term as we had other children. You cannot wait until the baby cries; you have to dream feed them for them to get out of the habit of waking for food. We have never fed a baby awake.*

This worked for ALL five of my children without issue, but you have to be strict and, like I said, alert to recognise the signs of them starting to stir for milk to prolong with the dummy. It's worth it!

***

GETTING OUT

We're sounding like a broken record, but please get out. Try it. Have the changing bag ready and go – and don't forget to either feed them first or have whatever equipment you need to feed them when you're out! The twins' groups are a great start – supportive and helpful and guilt-free. Or go for a walk. Try your local children's centre. If you are really struggling with this and feeling isolated and unsupported, speak to your health visitor and try Homestart if you haven't already. Don't forget time with your partner if you have one too, a cup of tea together and a change of scene can make the world of difference.

Postnatal depression, both in mothers and fathers, can come on at this period and so it is important to speak to your health visitor or GP if you are feeling tearful and low or increasingly anxious or not sleeping well (even if the babies are asleep).

You may feel jealous and stressed that some of your friends with one baby are going out and joining classes such as music or baby massage – unfortunately there is no getting away from the fact that this is much harder for twin mums. Maybe there is a mum of a single-ton mum who could help you? Or consider joining an online class. Honestly, the babies are still really small and there is a lot of time for this when the babies will appreciate the sessions more than the parents. Meeting other twin parents with older babies can be really help-ful and reassuring, so start by getting out to meet other parents or friends – it doesn't matter if you have not had a shower or have vomit on your shoulder – you will not be alone in your dress code. Other parents of multiples are also the most relaxed people about babies crying and will always have spare wipes, nappies, for-mula, vests, shoulders to cry on – whatever you need!

***

Elna

From day one I was out and about, but you have to be when they have an older sibling. I would say, whenever you come back, restock the nappy bag so it won't delay you for get-

ting out the next day. *My standards have dropped a bit – my first child was immaculate – but as long as they aren't stinking of poo they're good to go.*

Don't be afraid. I really do believe what you put your mind to you can do – it just takes a little bit longer. But it's really important to get out, you just have to get used to doing things a lot quicker.

***

Eleanor
I wasn't out and about until at least six weeks – they were born in February and also I'd had a Caesarean. Around week seven or eight I got myself together and got up and got out.

***

WHAT'S IT REALLY LIKE?

Get ready for some crying – them and you. There will be many battles – to get them to sleep, to stop yourself from going to sleep and between partners when one has gone back to work and does not understand how exhausted and upset the parent at home is. But the smiles, the chuckles, the way you can see their whole face light up when you enter the room, will lift your heart and see you through.

Try to get as much help as you can, and if caring for them is just too much or their smiles aren't lifting you as you think they should, reach out to family, friends and other parents – and maybe get to the GP.

***

Hugh (Ella's husband)

There will be times when you feel you need a break and they will inevitably occur at the same time that your partner needs your help the most. So, plan ahead and agree before the babies come to have some protected time for yourself and for your partner, and don't forget that time together with the babies is not the same as time alone.

Chapter 7: Three to Six Months

A lovely age – full of smiles and giggles – and the first glimpses of your babies interacting with each other will make your heart melt. You will start to see their individual personalities develop, and if you have identicals you will find it easier to tell them apart – well, on most days. Your day should now become more structured with feeding getting easier and cluster feeding stopping, and you can enjoy socialising again. If your babies have been ratty in the late afternoon or 'colicky', this is the time you will probably start to see a big difference and the light at the end of those long afternoons and evenings. Make the most of this time before solids come in and wreak havoc around your house once more (and not for the last time).

EQUIPMENT TO ENTER THIS PERIOD WITH:

Additional cot if you've only been using one so far

Peekaboo and lift-the-flap books (can be borrowed from the library)

Basic toys, especially noise-makers (empty containers with lids with uncooked pasta inside make great rattles for starters)

DEVELOPMENT

At three months (correcting for any prematurity) your babies should have good head control and, if they have had some practice at tummy time, you will notice they start liking time on their fronts, lifting up their heads, holding their weight on their forearms or outstretched arms and looking around. They start to reach out and grab at around four months (now you know what the rattles are for), may start to roll around at four to five months, start to transfer from one hand to another by six months and start to coo, blow raspberries and eventually go on to babble. They start to interact, noticing each other and developing their own individual characteristics and personalities – it really is a joy unique to having twins.

Some babies can sit with support at around five to

six months, but don't try to rush this. They need to develop at their own pace. When both are able to sit without support (usually by about seven months) they generally adore playing with each other and babbling to one another and you no longer have to be holding them – you have your hands back! Now you get a glimpse of how they may play together when they're older, while your friends will still be entertaining their singleton babies and toddlers.

However, while some babies make clear developmental steps, this can also be a tense and anxious time if you are worried about one or more of your babies' development. You may have multiple appointments with health professionals which can be very stressful.

***

Beatrice

It takes all my energy to go to the hospital – perhaps it reminds me of some bad memories. He [my baby] sees a dietician every two weeks, a speech therapist comes regularly, and I have seen a physio twice and have exercises to do at home. He had a developmental assessment done as well. I need organisation and time for appointments and it is exhausting.

Maybe psychological help might be good for me, but it

would be hard. I have no time for myself. With just twins I would have no time for myself. But I have four kids and one of them has health needs. So, I just have no time. There is also a financial element for us as I am not working and it is all on my husband's shoulders, so I cannot afford to see a psychologist.

***

SPEECH

Between three and six months, babies first start to make some recognisable 'happy' and 'unhappy' sounds, and will start to speak back to you in various different coos and babbles. They will turn their heads to listen to you when you speak to them as they love the sound of your voice – as well as the birds singing and rattles and scrunching up paper or foil. They will also love to turn pages of books and play peekaboo. Delight in their attention and they will delight in yours.

Try to talk to your babies individually as much as you can, and read to them at least at bedtime. Language development is generally slower for twins, likely down to them getting less eye contact and one-to-one time with adults compared to singleton babies and spending more time with each other as fellow non-speakers. It's not just down to you – encourage everyone who comes into contact with the babies to speak to them individually, it's lots of fun and will benefit them enormously.

SLEEP AND ROUTINE

Generally, daytime and bedtime routines will make more sense now for both you and your babies. Cues such as a bath, a story and a calming feed before bed will start to make a big difference as your babies will understand more and protest less. At this age, babies start to appreciate having punctuation points to their day – one of their naps in the buggy, a feed in a particular spot during the day at around the same time – and they will surprise you with how much they relax when words, actions, songs and timings become more regular.

WHERE ARE THEY SLEEPING?

At around three to four months your babies will have outgrown their Moses baskets and can now share a cot, if they are not already doing so. Babies can usually sleep head to head at this point, with their feet at the bottom of the cot on either side.

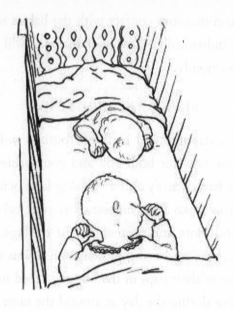

DAYTIME NAPS

Usually babies need fourteen to fifteen hours of sleep in total at this stage, with four to five hours of that being in the day. At three to four months, babies are more responsive to routines set by their parents but are often not biologically ready to sleep through the night (technically, this means sleeping for eight to twelve hours straight without night-time feeding). Around three months, your babies may be awake for three hours or longer in between naps, and may drop to three naps from four – a morning nap, an early afternoon nap and a late-afternoon catnap (lots of mums find this last nap easier to achieve out and about in the buggy rather than in cots). There is a growth spurt around six months at which time babies commonly drop down to two big daytime naps, totalling three or four hours altogether, with one nap in the morning and one in the early afternoon. Some people like a big morning nap for their babies and a smaller afternoon one to coincide with school pick-ups, but others prefer the reverse. Nothing is set in stone. However, once your babies have dropped their late-afternoon nap, you may need to bring bedtime forwards to 6:30 p.m. as they will be tired.

***

Lucia

I started with their routine at around three and a half months. I think for the first few months you can't really keep to a routine – they tell you it's baby led. At the beginning we decided that my husband would do some evening feeds but it didn't really work out so we started a different schedule – we woke them up at six every morning because we thought that if we establish the time they wake up we could get a routine for the rest of the day. And it worked really well: milk first and then when they were big enough for food and weaning we got breakfast at eight-fifteen, back into bed at nine until ten to ten-thirty, have their lunch at about twelve-thirty more or less, back to sleep around two and wake up at four, have their fruit in the afternoon and then dinner at six and in bed at seven, seven-thirty maximum. We're still holding on to that routine and it works pretty well for us.

Elna

Our babies started to sleep through consistently at eighteen weeks. For me with the twins it felt like an eternity because the first time it happened was around twelve weeks. I've always had them in quite a strong routine so my advice for twin mums is that's essential – I don't know how you cope with two babies without having a routine. In the early days it was feeding, bath and bed – I've always had that structure. I always fed them together, whoever woke up first then the other got woken up. My daughter was always waking up at 9 p.m., so she got an extra feed every night for the first few months. But during the night time they were always on the same time.

***

GETTING THEM TO SLEEP

Naps can cause stress if you are desperate for both

babies to go down at the same time at home so you can get a short break. Commonly, one of the naps can be achieved on the move either through necessity for other children or your sanity, but for the lunchtime nap (usually the longest) nearly all the parents we know would use their cots at home. The morning nap is commonly easier to manage than the lunchtime one so some parents separate the babies for their lunchtime nap if they really want it to work and be lengthy. You could use a travel cot or a pram for one downstairs or in another room. That way you can respond to one twin without waking the other.

As mentioned in the previous chapter, a good, simple tip is to introduce the naps in the same way each time by always putting them into a Grobag or with the same blanket, using a phrase such as 'it's sleep time' or 'naptime now' and using a light projector or song that plays every time you put them down – it all helps. They may start to roll over in their sleep but have not mastered rolling back yet – so this can also cause a few more wake-ups as they get stuck. They will usually learn to roll back themselves after a few days.

It's also worth re-emphasising the difference it can make to put your baby down in their cot *drowsy* instead of fully asleep – this means they actually learn to put themselves to sleep rather than you having to do it through feeding or rocking. Self-soothing is a very important skill for babies to learn and we both strongly believe that parents can help babies to develop this skill, calmly and without being strict about it. The problem is that if a baby is always rocked to sleep, if they wake momentarily or go into a lighter phase of their sleep cycle, they will wonder where their 'rocking person' is and then wake and cry – and this perpetuates the cycle. The same goes for sleeping on the breast. So, having a little gap between a feed and sleep, putting your baby down in the cot in a drowsy/tired state but not fully asleep, will eventually give you a baby who can self-settle and give you your time back.

It does mean you need to watch for cues to your baby getting tired and put them down before they are asleep, and before they are overtired as it will then be much harder for them to go to sleep by themselves. The Baby Whisperer series has a simple routine to follow and describes signs of tiredness to watch out for. Please note that this may seem impossible at first and take lots of picking up and putting down again – but it is worth persevering if you feel up to it.

If night-time sleeping isn't going well, you may start to think about sleep training at this point (although most parents we interviewed didn't try it until around six months). Common methods of sleep training are called 'gradual withdrawal' or 'rapid return' which lots of parents discuss online so you can follow their various success factors (or feel camaraderie with them for their efforts). If you have a partner sharing the night-time baby care, it is really important that they are fully on board with your chosen method and that you work on it together.

***

Katie

At five months they both slept through the night. From around four, four and a half months, they would take it in turns to wake up and I needed to get some sleep so I booked a night nurse. The night I called her is the first night they slept through the night. I hired the night nurse so I didn't have to get up in the middle of the night – they were waking around 3 a.m. (last feed at 10:30 p.m.) so it was one feed to get rid of. With two it's not like you can be up for twenty minutes for a quick little wake-up, it's an hour and then you've got to change their nappies.

Jibecke

Our two started sleeping through the night at four months.

We woke them up at ten-thirty every night and gave them a feed, until five months. We started realising that they weren't necessarily hungry when they woke up so then I wouldn't feed them straight away. Also, my mum advised us early on that if they wake up, before you pick them up, just touch them and see if that helps to settle them.

Amber

At six months we moved them out of our room and we put them into separate cots and they did not sleep, they didn't like it. It was weeks and weeks of this until by about eight months we couldn't do it any more, couldn't function, couldn't work as we were both getting up all the time. So, we went to a company that had been recommended to us and they advised us to follow the gentle retreat method. So, when they woke up, we had to hold their hand, then step away for a bit, then gradually move out the door, and that really, really helped.

***

Dummies and self-soothing

Dummies are very commonly used by twin parents and can be a big help to self-soothe. Muslins or soft toys designed for infants can also be used instead of, or in addition to, dummies. Making them smell of mummy by wearing them inside your top for a bit can help the babies want to snuggle with them.

The flip side is the issues caused by dummies or comforters: babies can become reliant on them. Woe betide anyone who loses them – and they can spawn a new nightly routine of dummy patrol as they fall out, the babies lose track of them and need you to get up and pop them back in. Once they are a bit older, they will be able to find it and put it back in but not yet. So, you may decide to remove the dummies and go cold turkey – it will likely take a couple of days for the babies to settle themselves without dummies. It is usually much quicker than you fear and certainly easier to remove at this stage than when they are older.

***

Ella

My twins stopped using their dummies around four months of age – the girls kept pulling them out but were not at a stage where they could put them back in and it was driving me crazy! So, I switched the dummy for a muslin and within two naps the girls never wanted them again. I imagined it would be war for days but within a day they had stopped complaining. The key was giving them the muslin

*and also making sure they were exhausted when they went
down to sleep.*

***

FEEDING

By now, we dearly hope you are all in great routines
that work for you and the babies. However, we realise
this is often not the case for many totally valid reasons.
However daunting it might seem, we would always
recommend you try to ease yourself into a routine
even if your first attempts didn't work out – now
would be as good a time as any to start again with bedtime or tackle a naptime that seems to work best at the
moment for all of you and go from there.

Around this time, breastfed babies will often be
feeding every three hours in the day but going for
longer and longer stretches between feeds at night;
possibly with a feed around 10:30/11 p.m. and then
one more wake-up the other side of midnight before
waking again in the morning. The feed during the
night becomes later and later and will slowly approach
morning time. Babies on formula are usually fed
roughly every four hours during the day (e.g. 7 a.m.,
11 a.m., 3 p.m., 7 p.m., 11 p.m.) with, again, a longer

stretch at night, perhaps from the late-night feed at 10:30/11 p.m. to 7 a.m. by four months.

The 'dream feed' seems to work well for a lot of families: if there are two adults around, the babies have a feed around 6:30/7 p.m. and then go to sleep. Mum (usually) goes to bed early and then her partner feeds the babies at 10:30/11 p.m. when they are semi-awake, using either formula or expressed breast milk. This hopefully means only one wake-up the other side of midnight, and this feed slowly draws nearer to 6 a.m.

NIGHT FEEDS

You may want to start to think about which feeds are habit and which are nutritional, and then cut back some of the habitual ones. There are different methods for cutting down on the feeds: some parents give the babies a dummy instead of a feed, some use water instead of milk, some use watered-down formula and some just stop. Obviously, only do this if you are confident and comfortable with your babies' weight gain.

***

Emily
I got mine to sleep through the night by gradually eliminating [bottle] feeds. I gradually moved the midnight feed

from 1 a.m. to 2 a.m. and so by fourteen weeks they were having a feed at 2 a.m. and then another little feed at 5 a.m. I started reducing the 2 a.m. feed by an ounce each night until it was gone. They stopped waking at 2 a.m. Now I had babies sleeping from 7/7:30 p.m. to 5 a.m., and to me that is a marathon of sleep which I as a mum could now get!!

So how to get rid of the 5 a.m.? Again, I started to reduce this feed by an ounce each morning until it was down to 2.5 ounces. This was fine for my daughter but my son was not impressed. So, I tricked him. I switched his fast-flow teat for a newborn slow-flow teat so he sucked for longer and harder. He thought he was getting more than he was. At seventeen weeks (while on holiday I might add) my daughter decided not to wake for this 5 a.m. feed and has never done so again. My son, Mr Fussy himself, followed suit three days later. It was nearly a more joyous moment than the day they arrived into the world!

No magic wand or Baby Whisperer secrets. Just persistence and following the same routine with a little bit of trickery along the way.

***

BREASTFEEDING

Whilst the bottle-feeding mums – let's be honest –

may be benefiting from a little more sleep than the exclusive breastfeeding mums, if you are breastfeeding at this stage you should be enjoying a nice routine of faster, less frequent feeds and often less winding, and all the other well-documented benefits of breast milk.

However, babies start to get more distracted during feeding around four to five months, and this can be difficult if you are out and need to feed as they want to turn and look around. Try to find somewhere quiet or time feeds in between outings if this becomes problematic. This distraction during daytime feeds can mean they don't get enough milk and start to wake up more at night to feed (this is called sleep regression) – so do try to keep feeds as calm and productive as possible.

It is a fact that by three months the majority of twins are not being breastfed, for a whole variety of reasons. Remember, the key thing is to do what works for your own mental and physical health and for your babies.

If you have a lot of support, if you've breastfed before or if you come from a family who breastfeeds, these are all positively linked to continuing breastfeeding. If you are keen to continue to breastfeed and don't have support or experience around you, try to find another twin mum who has breastfed – she may give you the moral support you need and practical tips for keeping it up. Some mothers are now also preparing to return to work and may need to get their babies to take more bottles in the day but may continue to breastfeed before and after work.

If you are cutting back on breastfeeds or wanting to stop entirely, remember to do this slowly to avoid mastitis – most women can usually drop a feed every three days without too much discomfort.

SOLIDS

Some parents will start introducing solids at around five months of age (actual age, not corrected age). This is dealt with in more detail in the next chapter as, at the time of writing, NHS advice is to give only milk for the first six months. However, paediatricians often recommend early weaning if your babies have reflux, as solids will help with that. Officially, early weaning can be from seventeen weeks (actual age), if the babies are able, but most start later than this. You can ask your health visitor for information on this and see if there are any weaning workshops at the children's centres or health clinics.

GETTING OUT AND ABOUT

As your babies approach the six months mark, they will be feeding much more quickly and will be able to stay awake for longer – maybe two to three hours at a time – so you will need something to do. You might be able to time a trip just after a feed (and a poo if they usually have a bowel movement after a feed), knowing you'll have a good hour to walk to the shops or to a park. You may have even managed a shower and washed your hair whilst your babies are having their morning nap – clean clothes too (you can dream).

Take the babies out in slings if you have mastered tandem babywearing or two slings with two adults, as from three months they can face forwards and delight in seeing the world. Remember to go to your lovely twins' groups, make some friends and get some moral support – it's astounding the relief you can feel at being in a roomful of crying babies! Look for recommendations of baby music, signing and sensory classes – Louise found one run by a twin mum (although her twins were in their twenties) who was, unsurprisingly, very accommodating and understanding of a bit of extra fuss and noise coming from her corner of the room. That said, the babies won't benefit all that much from these activities yet – a walk under some trees and a CD of nursery rhymes will be really stimulating for them.

***

Rachel

When you meet other twin mums it's quite a club. There is a mutual understanding that's different from mothers of children of different ages and an immediate bond. I have a friend who had twins a week after me and we decided to meet up regularly – having someone who was going through the same thing as me was incredibly helpful and she was already a mum, so then we had different perspectives – we had a lot of exchanging tips.

***

FINALLY FOCUSING ON YOU

In all the hustle and bustle it is so easy to forget time for yourself and for you and your partner. We have all done this. Your life as an individual and as a couple with interests outside of nappies and milk and rattles needs attention. If you have never left your twins with someone else – a partner or grandparent or friend – it might be during this period that you try it, even for half an hour. A walk or a fitness class or a coffee – try it and see how it goes. It usually ends better than you think it will. Maybe you will arrive back to chaos but you'll be better able to cope when you've had some time to recharge your batteries.

Perhaps you might consider an evening out – not too far as to be worrying. Perhaps a relative could babysit just for a couple of hours so you could go for a pizza at lunchtime. For those of you with partners, your sex life may well have been put to one side – and your libido as a parent of twins can be something of a distant memory. You are not alone; it may take time to return and get back to normal (albeit slowly!). But… before you get carried away, remember contraception!

For your physical and sexual wellbeing, it is also important to remember your pelvic floor at some point and check it still exists – try to do those exercises on the sheet you were given in antenatal classes that has disappeared amongst the other bits of admin you have never managed to get round to. If there are *any* problems with incontinence or *any* pain during sex then visit your GP and don't live with it in silence – a women's health physio will help with all of these things and can work wonders.

Around this time, postnatal depression is still something to be wary of and remember – there is no need to feel embarrassed about it and, again, it is very important to speak to someone such as your GP or health visitor if you are affected. The sleep deprivation and possible isolation may take its toll. It is understandable and it is common, so speak out and you will realise you are not alone. There are some wonderful support groups that you can find through your GP or local children's centre. Sometimes anti-depressants are prescribed; this is usually for a short time in your life and can make the world of difference to you. Remember, too, postnatal depression can affect partners as well, who often live with it in silence, and it is important that we recognise it and seek help.

WHAT'S IT REALLY LIKE?

Your babies will be more engaging and robust, you will be more confident as a mum (nappy changing will take seconds, feeds will be much reduced) and hopefully your routines will be established, making it easier for you to get out and about. The chuckles and smiles and coos are so rewarding and the babies so cuddly at this age, it's wonderful – and you might even get the space to pat yourself on the back a little, thinking 'I made this adorable pair!'

For those who have managed to get their babies to sleep through the night, some semblance of mental normality will return, but for those that haven't (and it can be totally unrelated to anything you're doing) you will still be feeling – frankly – a little unhinged and wild-eyed after six months of it. Reach out for help, whether you're lucky enough to get someone to give you a night off or even if it's half an hour from a friend for a walk around the block with NO ONE ELSE TOUCHING YOU OR NEEDING YOU FOR ANYTHING (Louise can remember this feeling well).

To summarise with some terribly mixed metaphors, this age can be where you glimpse the light at the end of the tunnel, but you might also see yourself rapidly approaching the end of your tether. Keep reaching out for help and remember you are doing an amazing job, even when it doesn't feel like it.

***

Rob (Louise's husband)
Our first holiday was when George and Alice were about six months old, through necessity really as my parents lived in a small village in Devon. We stayed in a self-catering apartment which was separate to the rest of a bed and break-fast, which was a relief – our wake-up/breakfast and bed-times and noise levels were pretty unorthodox. We followed the same routine we had at home but being somewhere else

*felt like a break in some sense although, to be frank, it's still
a total blur!*

Chapter 8: Six to Nine Months

These months involve a different kind of joy as the babies' personalities shine through, and a different kind of exhaustion as your babies sit up, start solids and very possibly get mobile. It may also be the time when you feel enough is enough in terms of sleep deprivation, so read on for tips and shared experiences.

EQUIPMENT TO ENTER THIS PERIOD WITH:

Wipe-clean bibs (2 x each child) – ones with small necks to protect clothes

Long-sleeved waterproof bibs (2 x each child) – neoprene or machine-washable fabric

Beakers (ideally free-flow, with lids; 2 x each child)

Weaning spoons (3 x each child – one for you, one for them, one for the floor)

Ice cube trays/freezer bags

Highchairs – cheap and cheerful and easy to clean

Bouncer chairs – useful for weaning before babies can sit independently

Door bouncers

Toys: nursery rhyme CDs, board books, bath toys, shakers

A good weaning book

A plastic sheet to catch falling food

Baby toothbrush and toothpaste

Contraception

FEEDING: WHEN TO START INTRODUCING SOLIDS

If you're anything like the mums we surveyed, there is a good chance you'll start your babies a little earlier than the recommended six months when it comes to purées and porridge. Current UK health guidelines suggest not to attempt to wean before seventeen weeks (as the babies won't be ready), and not to leave it later than twenty-six weeks (both for nutritional and developmental reasons). When to start is slightly more complex for premature babies but, on the whole, it is six months 'actual age' i.e. six months from the time they were born, even if that means they are only four months old developmentally (i.e. corrected age). Some start earlier than six months but others may not be physically ready. For all babies, look for these signs of readiness: good head control, loss of tongue thrust (when they poke the food back out at you with their tongue) and showing interest in your food. If in doubt discuss with your GP, health visitor or paediatrician.

One good reason to start earlier than six months, other than your confidence of their readiness, is reflux (it helped enormously for Ella's twins). But if you're starting in the hope that it will make your babies sleep longer through the night (like Louise did), be prepared for it not to make any difference (it didn't).

Your health visitor and local children's centre may well have a free weaning workshop you could attend and will also give you great basic advice on dos and don'ts. The main headlines are no whole nuts, no honey, no runny eggs and avoid certain types of fish such as shark and swordfish whilst limiting others such as tuna. Avoid adding salt and sugar to baby foods. Cow's milk should only be used in cooking, not used as a drink. All of this and more will be covered in any good weaning book and all the good baby websites.

Purist baby-led weaners who hand over the family dinner definitely shouldn't start until they are very confident that all the signs of readiness are in place. This type of weaning involves spoon-free finger food and adult food, so it is really important that the babies are sitting up and interested. But, as with most other topics, us multiple mums seem to take the best of both worlds and combine purées with finger foods pretty much from the off.

The pros of purées and porridge are that you can usually get the babies to eat some of it and it's easy to see how much they are getting. There is also a lot less mess than when you hand over those well-boiled spears of organic tenderstem broccoli to be lassoed around their heads. A meal can be over and done with relatively quickly, even if you feel like you're getting repetitive strain injury with your spooning hand. But it does mean extra work as you are often making food separately for the babies rather than using your family meals. Mind you, there is nothing wrong with purée-ing your side veg dishes, as long as you separate out the babies' portion before adding salt to the remainder.

The big upside of introducing finger foods early, especially for two impatient, hungry babies, is that the babies can start to feed themselves. Patience is not a familiar virtue for a seven-month-old who really, really likes mashed banana, so handing it over can make for a happier baby. Put your plastic sheet or even newspaper down to make cleaning the floor easier, make yourself a cup of tea and let them get on with a plate of soft carrots, slices of tender chicken breast and some large pasta pieces – it's not only nutritious, it can also be highly amusing. It will be messy, but then all good things are. And there's nothing wrong with spooning in some pudding after their main course, especially if you think more of the food went onto the floor or into your mouth than into theirs.

Be brave when you start – one meal a day for a week, then two for a week and then three by the third week – this may take a little longer if you start earlier than six months. And at first a meal may only be a couple of spoonfuls or equivalent. Try to stay relaxed. Your babies are learning a new skill and, in most cases, you will be well guided by their appetites.

***

Amber

I didn't know anything about weaning. I didn't even know that babies ate proper food. I'd just got all the milk routine sorted when my NCT group started asking, 'When are you going to start weaning?' What? No way! So then I had to read another book and everyone said I had to get the

Annabel Karmel book. I didn't know about baby-led weaning so I didn't even have a choice – I just got to mixing up purées and started feeding them. I didn't have a clue then that I had to get into another routine of introducing food, but I would give them a couple of carrot sticks and broccoli or cheese whilst getting things ready. But I still found it hard.

Katie

I waited until six months; I didn't really see the need to start earlier so I kept them on milk for as long as I could. I did purées initially and we went through different foods quite quickly. I would try a new food in the morning and within a couple of weeks they were eating pretty well. By about seven to eight months I started making sure I was adding finger foods – they are good at picking them up and throwing them!

Jo

Because their reflux was so bad, we weaned them at four months. I think weaning is a bit overhyped – just give them food and they get on with it. We did a combination of purées and finger food for every meal and it was fine. I found it very messy and it's quite tedious, especially having to throw rejected morsels away, but that phase passes pretty quickly.

Elna

I loved it! I really liked weaning apart from the fact I cooked everything homemade, everything organic. It's a huge amount of food you're cooking and going through. The ice cubes of food in the freezer went down so fast! But they took to it quite well. Once you've got your logistics sorted then it's just fun – I really loved it, it was really cute. I had them sitting side by side in their highchairs with one big bowl and one spoon, shovelling it in, taking turns whilst my eldest sat next to me having his dinner. But it took them a lot longer to use a spoon and fork than my eldest did. Even now they're not using their cutlery – they use their hands a lot.

Vic

Solids was great because that was when the reflux finally stopped. We started as soon as we could at six months and that was life changing. It added a new level of logistics into the day; we made up loads of purées and froze them into ice cube trays and they ate everything we gave them! Sometimes the looks on their faces were hilarious but they enjoyed it. They started really putting on weight consistently so I look back on that as a really positive moment.

***

A note on nappies

Get ready for lots of nappies – interesting nappies of many colours. After what you will now remember as the bliss of milk-only nappies, solids nappies can come as a bit of a shock to all your senses, as well as your bins or laundry. You'll be washing your hands a lot, so you may also want to invest in some hand cream.

WHAT SHOULD THEY BE EATING?

Good introductory foods include soft fruits and cooked root vegetables. Ice cube trays are a great way of storing homemade purées in the early days, and you can pop out the frozen cubes and store in freezer bags to save space. Protein is very important, for example fish, chicken, cheese, baked beans (low salt/sugar), lentils, tofu – make sure you are introducing small amounts of these after your initial trial days, and then aim for a protein element in two meals a day. This may well aid sleep! Another important nutrient, iron, should now be coming from food and not just milk, so it is important to provide your babies with iron-rich foods such as green vegetables, baked beans, tinned sardines and red meat.

Add texture early as well as upping the finger foods – by nine months you should be mashing food very roughly, leaving big lumps. Aim to move on from fork-mashed to minced to grated to chopped by twelve months. Moving from purée to lumpy food is a key stage in their development – they need this to develop their speech muscles and also because if you leave it too long, your babies may refuse lumps and gag on them. So, get in early with lumps and be brave. If you are worried about choking, find a local paediatric first-aid course you can attend or speak to your health visitor.

Most of the twin mums we talked to made use of good-quality ready-prepared baby food, especially when out and about. However, it's worth noting that some brands make very smooth mixes that always contain fruit purée or juice so they may sound savoury but are actually very sweet – babies wolf them down, but it means that they may become accustomed to the texture and taste and so giving them a plain or cheese omelette may prove difficult down the line. A good tip when you are using ready-made food is to only open one sachet or packet of [overpriced, organic] baby food at a time, as one sachet is often enough for two babies, especially if you're supplementing with a few breadsticks whilst you're getting dinner prepared. You don't even need to heat them, although some babies will prefer warmed food.

Most children sail through weaning, enjoying different food groups and flavours. A minority of children will develop allergies to certain foods, varying in degree of response, from an itchy rash to diarrhoea or vomiting or a flare-up of eczema to a severe allergic response called an anaphylactic reaction. Common foods that cause an allergic response include fish, eggs, nuts, kiwi and strawberries. Do not automatically avoid these foods but, obviously, if you have severe allergies running in your family then be mindful when trying them and by all means talk to your doctor. If your child starts to react and becomes itchy or blotchy with hives but has no problems with breathing or swelling, make an appointment with your GP to discuss diet and possible remedies for reactions, such as antihistamine syrup, which is only available on prescription for babies younger than twelve months. If they have any difficulty in breathing, seem unwell or have facial swelling, call 999.

For recipe ideas and more information on weaning methods, the following books are great for recipes and meal plans:

Feeding Your Baby and Toddler by Annabel Karmel – excellent meal planners at each stage

Baby-led Weaning: Helping Your Baby to Love Good Food by Gill Rapley and Tracey Murkett

River Cottage Baby and Toddler Cookbook by Nikki Duffy

Many of the above also have good websites and forums. Another good website is infantandtoddlerforum.org

HYGIENE (AND LACK THEREOF)

All feeding equipment should be sterilised for babies up to six months of age but, from then on, only bottles and teats need sterilising until 12 months of age; all the other feeding equipment like plates, spoons, cups, etc., can instead be washed thoroughly by hand or in a dishwasher. If your baby was born prematurely, usually you can apply this guidance to their actual age, rather than their corrected age, but with one caveat – if your baby has recurrent infections or at increased risk for infections, it is best to ask your health visitor or GP or paediatrician about when they recommend stopping sterilising bottles/teats and other feeding equipment.

If there are not massive differences between your babies in terms of weight and intake, most mums end up using one bowl and one spoon for both of them – they will definitely be sharing many other licked and sucked toys and food as well as utensils.

Hard plastic or wooden highchairs (Ikea for the budget option, Stokke for blowing the budget) are much easier and faster to clean than padded ones. Long-sleeved bibs with well-fitting necks are great when starting out – either easy to clean in the sink or machine washable. There may be a lot of food and water going in unexpected places (so remember an apron for you too).

DIFFICULTIES

The main source of stress when introducing solids is the babies not eating. But unless there are issues with weight gain which need to be addressed with your GP, remember that they will be getting pretty much all the nutrition they need from their milk. You'll have a lot on your plate without obsessing over whether it was two or three spoonfuls of papaya that Thing One had whilst Thing Two only had one. A good rule of thumb is if they eat it, good; if they don't eat it, freeze it or throw it in the bin. The ends of uneaten purées can go into soups for your lunch, or make great fruit sauce for yoghurts or ice cream.

Whilst it's lots of fun, it can also be another very tiring and isolating time as it seems impossible to leave the house with the endless cycle of cooking, feeding and clearing up. But once they've got the hang of a sachet and a rice cake, try to get out. It'll get you some amused looks and possibly offers of help that might turn into friendships if you go to a busy local café.

NB: given you'll need two highchairs, it might be best not to go at a regular person's mealtime.

***

Lucia

I think weaning was where I didn't have enough help and support. Although I could have asked, I'm sure. But the help wasn't there, it seemed. I was really, really afraid that they may choke – that was my biggest fear so I made sure everything was quite soft and they couldn't really choke on anything. But I think I overdid it in a way, so they are not that used to chewing. One of them seems to be swallowing more than chewing even now (at eighteen months). That is one thing I probably would change. I would get more advice on how to feed and wean them properly and a bit more help on going through my fears and overcoming them.

Beatrice

Thomas [born prematurely with a long stay in a neonatal unit] *has always had problems with feeding and a scan showed some fluid was going into his lungs, and so he has a nasogastric tube. He takes milk via the tube and purées by mouth. He used to vomit a lot. At times I don't feel like a mum – I feel like a nurse. I was coping well till all the tube feeding started and then I got burnt out. But now I'm better.*

Rachel

I found weaning really difficult. We started just before six months and they really struggled with the spoon. I think they were definitely interested and showing all the signs – interested in us when we were eating – but getting the food into their mouths took a good six weeks. I found this one of the most frustrating periods – when you prepare all this organic steamed veg purée then they eat absolutely nothing. Then all of a sudden – maybe by the time they were seven months – they got the hang of it quickly and were on to three meals a day.

Eleanor

I shudder when I think about it now – I can't say I particularly enjoyed it. It was fine really, but one of my two was much less receptive. I started earlier than current advice – at five months – which was probably a bit too late for my bigger girl as she was really hungry. But the smaller one wasn't quite ready so she spent two weeks rejecting everything I gave her, which was stressful. There's not much you can do if you're on your own and you're trying to feed two and it's difficult. What was nice was that my dad would come and help me in the late afternoon, and he could give one some milk whilst I was still feeding the other one. One pot with one spoon and the two of them next to each other is a key tip in terms of the practicalities of actually doing it.

***

MILK

As the quantity of food goes up, the babies' milk intake will reduce – this may take longer on the whole if weaning is purely baby-led. Whether you're breast-feeding or bottle feeding, you can begin to replace some feeds with snacks. Some mums will choose to change from stage 1 formula to a follow-on formula now, but sticking with stage 1 milk is also fine.

If you're breastfeeding, this might be the time you consider swapping out a feed for a bottle, or, if you've already done so, you can continue to do that with more of your feeds over the following weeks. Make sure you express only a little milk if your boobs get painful. If this is the right time for you to stop altogether, then, to avoid mastitis, don't drop more than one feed every three days. Get ready for feeling very emotional; breastfeeding does give some of us a hormonal high that's hard to give up (those bras won't be). Also remember that you may well become more fertile and start having periods (if they haven't started already) once you cut back on breastfeeds, especially night feeds. So, if you need to, start contraception again. (Note: you can still get pregnant whilst breastfeeding and even before you have a period.)

If you are switching to a bottle for the first time, the babies may struggle to drink enough milk from the teat, and they won't yet be getting enough calories from food if they have only just started solids. This can be tough going and a lot of perseverance is needed. One common trick is feeding them somewhere different or in a different position, such as in a car seat. As mentioned previously, try leaving the babies with your partner or a friend so they can have a go with the bottle. Mums will sometimes try a lot of different teats before one eventually works – teats that closely resemble the breast, such as MAM, tend to work best.

From around nine months of age, you might also find that they can get enough milk from a cup (in addition to some breastfeeds and dairy at mealtimes) thereby skipping the transition to bottles entirely – but it would be unusual for this to happen much before the nine-month mark. If you are returning to work around this time, the babies may take a cup of expressed breast milk or formula in the daytime, and you can still breastfeed before and after work. By this time they should also be on good amounts of solids, including dairy.

VITAMINS

In the UK, current recommendations are that babies who are breastfed should be given a multivitamin containing vitamin D from birth. Vitamin D is normally produced by our bodies using sunlight (what sunlight? you may ask! Exactly!) but in the UK there is insufficient sunlight to make enough vitamin D so babies need supplements. Vitamin D is needed for rapid bone growth and for the immune system. Babies who are formula fed need to start a multivitamin once they are on less than 500 ml per day (formula has enough vitamin D in it until then). You can get these from the health visitor, your GP or over the counter from a pharmacy. The Department of Health recommends you continue these daily until five years of age.

DRINKING WATER

Try to offer your babies tap water in a beaker (ideally free-flow, which can be messy) at every meal from six months onwards. The more you offer this, the more they will use it and stop drinking from bottles – normally at some stage around twelve months (as recommended by health visitors, although not set in stone). Some mums report that their babies get a little constipated when they start solids, and good water intake will help to prevent this from happening.

FEEDING ROUTINE

Here is a simple plan for food and milk at around six to seven months that works for lots of parents. Parents rarely stick to these kinds of plans rigidly, so feel free to adapt. It's here to be a help at what can be an overwhelming and busy time!

7 a.m. milk

8 a.m. breakfast – can be porridge mixed in with their usual milk and some fruit purée on top, or lightly buttered toast fingers with fruit pieces

9 a.m. nap

11 a.m. milk

12 p.m. lunch

12:30/1 p.m. nap

3 p.m. milk
5 p.m. dinner
7 p.m. milk
11 p.m. milk

You might notice the 11 p.m. feed starting to become shorter and the babies' milk intake decreasing. This late feed usually stops sometime around seven months. Babies rarely need milk overnight for nutritional reasons after six months.

By nine months, milk feeds should be down to 7 a.m., 3 p.m. and 7 p.m. on this plan (replacing the 11 a.m. milk feed with a snack).

It really can be exhausting, just muddling through from one feed to the next with a lot of mess, but if you keep trying with an increasing variety of textures, finger foods and some water in a beaker, your babies will really get it. Your life will be transformed – a rice cake or banana can keep them busy and they will be very entertaining to each other, the world and to you!

ROUTINES AND SLEEP

From six to nine months, babies sleep for fourteen hours out of the twenty-four, with about three to four hours in the day and the rest as hopefully unbroken sleep at night. Having a daytime and bedtime routine will help your babies sleep through the night; it's a fact.

You may well be utterly exhausted by this stage in their lives, but with a little more routine we hope you'll soon get some rest. According to the National Sleep Foundation, most babies (70 per cent) sleep through the night by the time they hit nine months. So take heart, and look at these ideas to help you get there.

NAPS

Naps are very important for night-time sleep; an over-tired baby will find it hard to relax at bedtime and a baby who has had too much daytime sleep will wake more at night or will wake up early. At six to nine months of age, babies can be awake for three to four hours at a time in between naps.

From six to nine months of age, babies usually have two to three naps ranging from forty-five minutes to 120 minutes. Some babies drop their third nap in the afternoon at around six months and need an earlier bedtime; others continue with a short catnap at around 4 p.m. for a while longer, but when they won't go down to sleep at bedtime (around 7 p.m., let's say), you know it is time to cut the later nap. Maybe five grouchy late afternoons should be the worst you'll have to go through.

Many books recommend trying to have the morning nap no earlier than 9:30 a.m., to avoid early rising. Commonly, twins have about forty-five minutes at 9:30 a.m. and two hours around 12:30 p.m. (after lunch). But don't worry if your two are not going by the books! At nine months, Ella's twins were having ninety minutes at 9/9:30 a.m. and another ninety minutes around 1/1:30 p.m. The main thing is to aim for at least one daytime nap of ninety minutes of unbroken sleep.

The lunchtime nap becomes very important because this is the one that stays until they are as old as three years. You may need to separate your twins to get it to work. Ella used to put one of her girls upstairs in her cot and the other downstairs in a travel cot. This way she could attend to one without disturbing the other, and soon they were both sleeping for ninety to 120 minutes at a stretch. With this pattern established, she then put them both back together in their room. Once they could roll back and forth, her girls liked to sleep on their tummies with their rabbit comforters close by and a music projector that went on for a couple of minutes before they nodded off. This way of sleeping lasted – and worked – for two years.

It can be hard to organise the nap routine, especially if you have an older child and school pick-ups; sometimes the babies fall asleep in the car or pushchair when you least want them to and this late nap in the afternoon can then interfere with bedtime. Try to have at least one of the daytime naps in the cot/s. If you have not yet done this, try to introduce a similar routine before each nap, such as a nappy change, a book and a cuddle with a consistently used phrase such as 'it's sleepy time now' – have a look back at the advice in Chapter Six.

Schedule the naps according to what works for you as a family, and you can shift them gradually – for example, you can delay a nap by ten to fifteen minutes every two to three days until you get to your desired time.

EXERCISE

It might sound daft for six-month-olds, but think about how much activity your babies are getting. If they are in their buggies or bouncy chairs all day without much stimulation, they will be napping a little on and off and not getting tired enough to have good naps and night-time sleeps. Parents usually report that babies sleep better after a baby group or play session at home – even if all they are doing is waving a toy around in time to music. So every day, make sure your babies have tummy time, have some play time with music and toys and go out in the buggy to give them a change of scene. This doesn't have to be expensive – a trip to the shops will be fascinating for them and gets you in touch with other grown-ups, and a peaceful walk through the park will be even more soothing for both of you.

BEDTIME

A bedtime routine at this stage, and hopefully for a while now, usually consists of a bath, possibly a massage, getting into night clothes, a feed, storytelling, a goodnight kiss and a cuddle. If your babies were having a split feed (i.e. having half their feed before the bath and half afterwards in their warm and dimmed room), they are probably no longer doing this as they are now having dinner before their bath, and can have their final milk feed after their bath, once they are ready for bed. After this, hopefully your babies will go down sleepy, but not fully asleep, in their cot. As discussed, this lets them soothe themselves to sleep. It's a good idea to have a bedtime story between the feed and bedtime as this helps to reduce any association between feeding and sleeping and reduces the chance of your babies falling asleep on the breast (which, at this stage, you are likely to be wanting to stop).

Dummies

Parents who have kept the dummies going find that, at around nine months, their babies can reach out and find their own dummies and pop them back in, which is a lifesaver. Some parents buy a cuddly toy that you can attach several dummies to, or have lots of dummies around the cot so that the baby can always find one in the night without you. One of Louise's twins didn't want a dummy and – you may think her mad, but read on – she introduced a dummy to the other twin at around six months. This was because he liked to be breastfed to sleep and a dummy helped him lose that habit. The dummy fairy (Google it) visited him when he was around two and a half to give the dummy to another baby and very kindly dropped off a gift for him and his sister as well.

TACKLING SLEEP

Over half of the mums we interviewed were getting

their babies to sleep for at least six hours by the time they were six months old – but some of these mums had the help of maternity nurses or some form of sleep training. There were still a significant number of babies who hadn't managed to sleep through the night at six months, Louise's included. This is a long time for an adult to be sleep deprived, so, unless you are totally happy with how life is going, it's probably time to think about tackling the sleep situation.

Mums of twins often bond over how irritating it is when mums of singletons talk about understanding sleep deprivation because their babies were poor sleepers – let's face it, a quick feed and a nappy change of one baby can take a dozy twenty minutes. For two, you may end up with at least an hour of activity and mum wide awake and wired for the next hour.

WHERE THEY SLEEP

The first thing to sort is the basics of where they are sleeping. At six months your babies no longer have to sleep in the same room as you and this transition may be the change you all need – you could be inadvertently waking up the babies. Or the babies could be waking each other up. Moving them into separate cots can really help. Failing that, and if feasible, different rooms for each baby may be what's required if only as a temporary solution. For example, Louise left her 'sleepier twin' in another room to snooze through the night whilst she attended to the more wakeful twin in a cot next to her bed. Practically speaking, it can be exhausting and overwhelming to try to tackle them both at the same time, especially if both are crying and there is only one of you, so separate rooms can be helpful for this reason. Being realistic, you may also need to play musical beds with your partner at this time, dependent on how much practical help they can give. Any form of sleep training is easier with two pairs of hands, however, so, if you have a partner or willing helper, this might be the time to ask for help (again).

NIGHT-TIME FEEDS

A common issue at this stage is weaning off night-time feeds, which may well have become a habit more than a necessity. Many mums find that it works well to space out any remaining overnight feeds by gradually reducing the milk volume (or time at the breast) at each feed over a couple of weeks, rather than going cold turkey. It's good to give them a good dinner of complex (slow-burning) carbohydrates, such as porridge (especially if you know they like it and will eat well). This way, you can be reassured that the babies are very unlikely to be hungry. That said, it didn't seem to make an enormous difference to Louise's babies' sleep habits.

OTHER REASONS FOR WAKING UP...

Once babies stop their night-time feeds, they might still wake up at night. It is important to make sure it is not due to hunger or a medical issue – and it usually isn't.

Are they definitely warm enough?

Adding another layer to what they are wearing can really help them sleep if the room is too cool (it should be between sixteen and twenty degrees C). If they are too warm, they are likely to try to kick covers off, but obviously this is worth checking as well, especially if they are in sleeping bags.

Teething, mild illness or discomfort

Your babies' first teeth usually appear between five and nine months. While some babies breeze through it, it can be really miserable for other babies and their parents. Between teething and a variety of coughs and colds, sleep can be very disturbed. For teething pain, over-the-counter pain relief designed for babies and small children, such as ibuprofen, probably work best. Teethers designed to be kept cold can also give instant relief, and parents also reported successfully using cold carrots, bananas and chilled flannels.

If you do have a tough period of teething or illness, do try to get some extra support in the day and get some rest, if you can. Sharing the load at night is also really helpful if at all possible. You may find you need to sleep near one of the babies if you are worried about them. Or, again, you may need to separate your twins in order for one (or someone) to get some sleep. Put one of them in a bathroom if you don't have space anywhere else! Try to keep up the bedtime routine throughout and give reassurance, but keep your babies in their own cots as far as possible (and not in your bed). After this period, things should go back to how they were and any routines you had established should start up again.

Other disturbances

Sleep can be disturbed for many other reasons, from you returning to work, to moving home, to taking a holiday, to clock changes, to transitioning from a basket to a cot (or cot to bed later on). Another developmental reason for disturbed sleep at the six-to-nine-month stage is that your babies may be able to stand in the cot but not sit themselves back down. Also, they might be moving around the cot and playing. Lots of parents also report little phases of wakefulness whenever their babies have any form of developmental spurt – it must be an exciting time for these little people. Thankfully, all these reasons for waking up should be short-lived. Keep the routine in place, keep your babies in their own beds and be reassuring but firm.

SLEEP TRAINING

Some parents get to a stage where they are so exhausted, seeing no way out of the sleep deprivation, that they call in a sleep trainer or follow a sleep training programme. Parents of multiples will be more likely to reach this stage earlier than those with one baby. These methods can be very successful, but if both twins are having problems sleeping, we recommend you tackle one twin's sleeping issues before you move on to their sibling – especially if you are on your own or if your partner is unable to help at night. We would recommend twins are in separate rooms for this period, to be reunited once everyone is sleeping! Importantly for those of you with partners, it is essential for both parents to be on the same page and ready to work together in order to be successful.

The most common sleep-training techniques are:

Controlled crying

This terrible-sounding method involves going into your baby's room at set intervals (e.g. one or two minutes), comforting them and going out of the room again. Once they seem to be settling themselves the intervals very gradually get longer. This technique commonly works within three nights. (Please don't confuse this technique with 'crying it out', when babies are left to cry for extended periods of time, which neither of us would advocate.)

Gradual retreat

This is where parents slowly move a little bit further away at each bedtime, sometimes over days and weeks, so the baby learns to fall asleep on their own. This is a gentle approach and can be a great way to avoid any crying, but it can take a long time!

Wake to sleep

Wake to sleep involves resetting your baby's body clock for early risers or for dealing with a clock change or jetlag. This involves gently disturbing the baby without waking them up an hour before their early wake-up time to try to reset their sleep cycle in the hope they will sleep for longer. It requires an early wake-up for you, but can be very successful in breaking habits. But if it hasn't worked after a few nights, you will need to try something else.

Talk through your issues with your health visitor (and GP) who is fully trained to deal with all kinds of sleep issues in babies and children, and can give you good guidance on reducing night feeds and awakenings. The Millpond Children's Sleep Clinic have published a good book called *Teach Your Child to Sleep*. It details common sleep problems and sleep-training techniques and provides several plans for each sleep problem. Other books on sleep which we recommend include *Healthy Sleep Habits, Happy Twins* by Marc Weissbluth and *The Sensational Baby Sleep Plan* by Alison Scott-Wright.

Also, get support, advice and recommendations from other twin parents through the various forums and groups we have outlined in the first chapter.

Beware of asking about sleep training in a general baby online forum as there may be lots of anti-sleep training 'trolls' ready to pounce!

Phrases such as 'controlled crying' may sound cruel but, correctly followed, may only mean leaving a child to cry for a matter of minutes (and twin babies are generally used to that). The reality is that many twin parents need to use some sort of sleep-training technique – even in its mildest form – and it can really help. Your twins will be used to waiting for and sharing your attention and crying a bit whilst doing so. In the end, your twins will be sleeping, sharing, waiting and being adoring and adorable, and no harm will come to them while allowing them the gift of sleep.

DEVELOPMENT

During this stage, babies will generally start sitting up unsupported, making their first recognisable language sounds (e.g. mamama), will laugh and smile a lot (at each other is adorable), transfer objects from one hand to another, blow raspberries, show increased stranger awareness and will sometimes start crawling or shuffling (although most do this from nine months). It is important to remember that, if your babies are born early, they may well reach their milestones at the right time according to their 'corrected' age (which takes into account any prematurity).

As mentioned in the last chapter, twins may have delayed speech – probably as a result of less one-to-one interaction and eye contact with adults compared to singletons, and also because some twins will have their own language (known as cryptoglossia). If they are learning two or more languages, this can also delay their speech, but it nearly always resolves itself – and how amazing to have two languages!

Within these months, your babies will also start to respond to their names – another good reason to ensure you get a little individual time with each baby. Bath time can be a nice time to do this, although having a double bath seat for when they can both sit up is very cool. And if there are any differences in naptimes, make the most of them and ensure that you're using their name and making lots of eye contact. This, along with reading to them, is the best way to encourage their language development at this age.

Take notes from parents and grandparents to find out if any of your relatives were early walkers or bottom shufflers, as it tends to run in families. Depending on how your babies' mobility is developing, you should probably start eyeing up your living space for baby proofing (how many wires can a crawling baby grab? How baby-safe are any other children's toys within reach?) and looking for stairgates. Many twin parents maintain their sanity (and home) by investing in a playpen (which Louise's son helpfully referred to as 'the prison' just to make her feel better about it).

Sitting up and picking up toys means that the tug-of-wars will start, but at this age there don't tend to be any battles. They will also learn to throw things (often the food you have painstakingly prepared) which can be highly entertaining for them, not for you, especially from a highchair...

It is important to speak to your health visitor or your GP if your twins are slow to reach these milestones; check your Red Book (Child Health Record) for milestones and write them down to keep as a memory and for health professionals if needed.

***

Martina
Ella was always desperate for Grace to interact and play but Grace wouldn't even look at her. Then about two weeks ago (eight months old) they just clicked and now they look at each other and just start laughing.

***

PLAY

At this stage the babies are interested in everything and everyone. Ella has vivid memories of her two sitting and communicating with each other in their own way before snatching the other one's toy. Plastic bottles can become shakers with the addition of rice or lentils. Saucepans can become drums. Anything goes. Music will be a favourite at this stage – try a CD with nursery rhymes (there are lots of compilations on YouTube too) or a noisy toy that plays a tune (those long-lasting batteries can be a blessing and a curse). Other items that work well include bath toys, books, balls, stacking cups and pop-up toys.

Door bouncers mean they see the world from a different angle and they can get a real thrill from the speed it allows them to move at. Crawlers will be into everything and will pick up objects from the floor, so it is important to move any potential choking hazards such as an older child's marbles or Lego out of reach. But don't worry too much about the state of the floor or being excessively clean – the developmental benefits of being allowed to explore outweigh the small risks of bugs from the floor. If you haven't managed to take a baby first-aid course yet, now would be a great time –

with additional mobility and interests come additional risks.

GETTING OUT

As well as thinking about your social life, it's time to go to the local library for Rhyme Time or the local children's centre for a stay and play session. Your babies won't be playing with other children or each other yet, but they will enjoy seeing lots of other people, listening to music and having new toys to look at and stick in their mouths (don't worry, playgroups will clean toys between sessions).

An important note on classes is that they also have to be enjoyable for you and not just the babies. Parents often gravitate towards things they enjoy (babies would enjoy most things) and that is fine as it is meant to be for you as well! Those who like singing tend to attend classes where they can sing, those who are creative may go to messy play; it really doesn't matter and isn't going to determine whether your child will be a concert pianist or a famous artist in the future (sorry). And don't feel guilty if you can't afford or don't have time or the inclination to do any classes at all.

But if you haven't had an evening out yet, make sure you arrange one – yes, we are nagging now.

***

Hugh (Ella's husband)

The challenges you will face are going to constantly evolve. For example, the babies will become more alert and therefore require more attention during the day. On the other hand, their night-time sleep will gradually improve so you will be more able to cope with the additional demands. So, plan date afternoons for when the babies are napping (don't always plan date nights – by night time all you want to do is sleep).

***

Things friends can do for you:

Prepare fruit and vegetable purées and freeze them in ice trays

Help with feeding and cleaning up (at home or going out with you to a café)

Take babies out whilst you have a nap

Bring children round to either play with your older children or to make your babies smile – they're becoming more fun for other kids to be around

Help out at bath time

CHILDCARE

If you are going back to work by twelve months you will need to be thinking about childcare now, working out logistics and budgets. Think about the kind of environment or care you want and ask about others' experiences and opinions before making a decision. It may be worth putting their names down at a nursery or childminder at this stage (even if you haven't visited them – you can always turn the place down if you decide that it's not for you – although some popular nurseries charge a non-refundable registration fee). Towards the end of this period, you may need to start interviewing nannies and meeting childminders if that's what you decide to go for. As a general rule, childminders usually end up being the cheapest option and mean your babies will be in a loving home environment. Nannies and nurseries usually end up costing around the same for two children, but each option has its own pros and cons. For example, you can't send a sick child to nursery, but can leave it at home with a nanny. On the other hand, if the nanny is sick, you will have to cover, whereas a nursery will arrange cover if one of their staff is under the weather.

When you are calculating your budget, remember to take into account that a nursery might cover some expenses such as nappies, food, activities and classes. On the other hand, care for older children will be covered by a nanny. We will cover these options in more detail in the next chapter. You might find that there are some experienced nannies looking for work as older twins start school, so it's worth asking around the other twin mums as early as possible, if this is the route you choose to take.

Even before you go back to work, you may also need childcare for specific times or tasks, so, again, start asking friends about the availability of their nannies or childminders, as you may be able to borrow a nanny for a couple of hours, or drop them off with a childminder for short periods of time.

***

Judith

Getting to hospital is difficult – I always have to go with someone. Parking is an issue. I have to park outside while someone stays in the car with the babies. I run in to get a permit, then with the permit I go and find parking. We can be waiting for hours – sometimes all day – to see all the different people we are seeing: orthoptist, nurses, ophthalmologists. Or we might be there for one baby and not the other, so I need to then pay for a nanny to come with me. It

*is really difficult and there's no other way of doing it. I don't
have family support around. It's expensive.*

***

OLDER SIBLINGS

There may seem little time to do anything other than
feeding till your babies have started to cut down their
milk feeds and can take some finger foods properly at
around eight to nine months. The knock-on effect is
less time with your older child. But have a think – do
I need to be there for every feed now? Can the twins
be left with someone else so I can have some time with
my older child? The key is to plan your time, write it
down on a calendar and stick to it – unless you do this,
something will always get in the way.

As the twins start to interact more and crawl
(between seven to ten months), they can be highly
entertaining for older siblings but they may also interfere with the older child's toys and this can cause temporary resentment, so it may mean creating a safe space
for your older child and their toys (as well as spending some special time with them). Ella remembers that
this was the first (not the last) time her eldest got angry
with his twin sisters – when they started getting into
his space and his toys. He was still so young that it

was hard to make him understand, or discipline him or use reward charts and so on. It took about a month of resentment before it dissipated, and the only thing that really worked was giving him his own space and his own time.

Try to factor in some special time with your older child, but don't beat yourself up about it or give yourself or your child impossible expectations of quite how special it will be. It doesn't need to be a big day out – it can be as simple as fifteen minutes of regular one-to-one time. Louise's husband used to drive her eldest son to a class every week, but they decided to switch so she took him on the bus while her husband gave the twins their lunch. From when Louise's twins were a few months old, their morning nap would be on this bus whilst she took her eldest to nursery and they would chat together, side by side. Now he's a lot older, a bus journey together is still one of the best times and places they have to discuss how his life is going and how he feels about the world.

***

Louise

When George and Alice were around eight months old, I was out for a walk with Thomas, my eldest son, aged three. Out of the blue he suddenly said, 'It's tricky, isn't it, Mummy?' to which I asked, 'What's tricky?' 'Now the babies are here,' he solemnly replied.

***

WHAT'S IT REALLY LIKE?

The start of weaning can be totally chaotic and stressful, but, if you're tolerant of a bit of mess and bold with finger foods, it can be lots of fun. Your house will become a lot more chaotic with bibs, nappies, bigger, louder toys and loads more clothes to wash, so take a deep breath if you are a very tidy, controlled person – this is a busy, messy time.

As the months go on, life will get easier; there is a much better chance you'll all be sleeping better and the babies will be able to be cared for more easily by others. This will allow you some time for yourself, your partner or other children. Gaze at them while they are asleep and enjoy those last night-time feeds (as for the vast majority of you, they will soon be a much-cherished memory). Now your babies start showing their preferences in food and toys, moving themselves about independently and develop into – frankly – much more interesting little people.

Chapter 9: Nine Months to One Year

You've nearly made it to a whole year and life will be so much easier. Your babies will be engaging with the world, may be moving independently and starting to communicate their wants and needs to you by means other than crying. It's likely they have teeth, are eating finger foods and will be amused by the world around them and the banana squished in their little hands. Looking back to the first few months will seem a lifetime away – you got through it! Luxuriate in how much more sleep you have (OK, some of you might still be grateful for a regular six hours, but many more will have a full night's sleep). Your babies will be fun. Make sure you spend some time just hanging out with them in these months and being amused by their different personalities shining through – especially if this is the time before you return to work.

EQUIPMENT TO ENTER THIS PERIOD WITH:

Stairgates (if you need them)

Playpen (or two)

Door jams, cupboard locks, socket covers, corner protectors

Walker toys such as basic trolleys with bricks

Very basic puzzles, lots of picture books

Crayons and paper

Forward-facing car seats (dependent on size)

Lightweight double buggy (optional)

Reins (optional)

FEEDING

By this stage, most babies will have milk in the morning, three meals during the day followed by milk at night before bed, with their 3 p.m. milk feed replaced by a snack. By twelve months, they can have milk in a beaker with breakfast and at night before brushing their teeth (although many will still have a bedtime bottle or breastfeed). At twelve months, although you may have already been incorporating cow's milk into food, your babies can now have milk as a drink instead of formula or breast milk, which for most makes life easier (but it must be full-fat milk until they are two).

Bottles should be phased out or cut altogether for the good of their developing teeth – official guidance is that they should not be using teats at all after one year. As previously mentioned, water in free-flow cups at dinner time is a great way to start, but, practically, you may need a non-spill sippy cup for buggies and car seats. Some babies will 'hold out' and not drink unless they get a bottle – if this happens, sadly, it's probably best to go cold turkey. That said, lots of people – including Louise – allow their babies a bottle at bedtime for a little longer, but make sure they are happily using cups at other times and do not leave them with their bottles in their mouths whilst falling asleep (milk does contain sugar, after all).

At nine months, make sure they are having the calcium equivalent of 600 ml of milk in their diet, including milk on cereal, yoghurts, cheese sauces, etc. (by twelve months, 350 ml is sufficient). At this age they should be trying various different finger foods and very textured foods such as crackers and bread sticks. It isn't necessary to buy the very expensive baby versions – plain unsalted rice cakes are cheaper and probably healthier than the baby versions sweetened with apple juice (although they may convince a very reluctant chewer!). Although most everyday bread products contain salt, unlike the baby versions, a little salt is OK as long as you are not adding salt to their food or giving them too many processed foods (such as baked beans and pre-prepared adult pasta sauces).

This is also a good time to introduce them to cutlery, if you haven't already – one spoon for them and one for you works well. You may find they are demanding you load up 'their' spoon rather than accepting the spoonful you're hovering in front of them. Some babies refuse to be spoon-fed at this stage (like Ella's) and you may need to accept the mess of them doing it themselves with their hands and spoons alongside finger foods.

At nine months, your babies should be enjoying a wide variety of proteins, carbohydrates and fruits and vegetables of various different textures. Your aim is to have your babies eating (still unsalted) cut-up adult food by twelve months.

REFUSING FOOD/DRINKS

Even if the introduction of solids went really well, food refusal can start at any time. For the vast majority of cases, it is fine to just weather it. Some will decide they don't like broccoli for a month then go back to it if you keep on offering it. When looking at your babies' diet, the best advice is to think about their whole week's intake of foods – don't worry if they don't eat much at one mealtime or get hung up on having three square meals a day with all the food groups represented at each sitting.

Of course, if there are pre-existing weight issues, discuss this with your health professional. If there are no allergies or digestive issues, try adding unsalted butter to vegetables and cream to puddings – it makes food more calorific as well as more appetising and fats are important for babies at this stage.

It's essential that they never get dehydrated, so if you need to stick with the bottles for a bit longer then that's OK. Don't panic too much if they are refusing to drink water but are getting liquids from milk, fruit and sauces. It's important not to get them used to drinking fruit juices as these have very little nutritional value and can be high in sugar, which is detrimental to their growing teeth and unhelpful to their developing palate. Drinking water is a fantastic habit to enforce. Louise occasionally treated her little ones to cooled fruit teas which have virtually no sugar, so this could be worth a try.

SLEEP AND ROUTINE

Having covered lots on this subject, we hope you are now seeing the light – you and your babies should be getting quality overnight sleep according to a routine you like and that works for all of you in the day. We hope this also includes time for socialising with your babies – with and without any older siblings – and also the occasional night out with your partner if you have one. Even if you are achieving just some of this, then you are doing brilliantly, you really are. It is all a 'work in progress'.

At nine months, babies usually have two daytime naps; one nap in the morning of forty-five minutes and another of one and a half to two hours after lunch. Sleep consultants mostly recommend that your baby is up by 3:30 p.m. so it does not interfere with bedtime. Between nine to twelve months the average daily nap-time should total two and a half to three hours. After twelve months, babies commonly drop the morning nap and have just the one long nap after lunch, two hours on average, which carries on until two to three years of age.

Sleep should become more predictable and more regular, and unbroken night-time sleep is hopefully taking place. Total sleep averages fourteen hours over a twenty-four-hour period. Sleep disturbances at night could be from teething, illness, standing up in the cot and moving a lot in their sleep. Don't rush to them as you will now find that they will settle themselves back to sleep, even after crying out a little. Keep to your routine as much as possible during these phases, as we said in the previous chapter. Other sleep disturbances include night terrors, snoring (which could be from sleep apnoea), and, as they get older, nightmares, sleep walking and sleep talking. *Teach Your Child to Sleep: Solving Sleep Problems from Newborn Through Childhood* by the Millpond Sleep Clinic details many sleep issues very well, but do discuss anything ongoing with your GP.

This is also a relatively common time to try sleep training if you haven't got an unbroken night's sleep yet. Whilst we wrote about the common methods for sleep training in the previous chapter, we wanted to acknowledge this and share a success story from one of our twin mum friends.

***

Ann-Marie

I decided to sleep train my twins at twelve months old. They started off being fantastic sleepers, waking for feeds and going back to sleep with no problems. Then, at about five months old, my girl twin decided that she could not settle herself to sleep any more and, petrified she would wake her brother, I decided to pick her up and rock her back to sleep or I would breastfeed her back to sleep. Then she started waking through the night and would only fall asleep on the breast, so she ended up co-sleeping with me.

When the twins were nine months old my husband passed away after a long illness. My breast milk stopped and I hoped Willow would be happier and fuller on a bottle, but she started to become even worse at night. I was surviving on four hours broken sleep a day. To say it was awful is an understatement. Teamed with my husband passing away and also having a nine-year-old to do the school run for each morning and doing 100 per cent of everything for me and the three kids every day, I was hitting breaking point.

Two days after my twins' first birthday I decided to go down the controlled crying route. It was either do that or have a breakdown – I was exhausted. So, I picked the twins up, said it was bedtime and walked them into the bedroom singing them a lullaby and lying them down.

I started off leaving them to cry for five mins, then went in to shush them, give them a pat on the back and lie them down again. I never spoke to them or made real eye contact. Then I increased the time to ten minutes, then went back in and repeated the process, then fifteen minutes. I never went past fifteen minutes of going in to check on them unless I could hear that they were falling asleep, if there were long intervals between crying or I could tell that they were just moaning in their sleep. Sometimes they would poo and that's why they were crying so I would change the baby in the darkened room whilst shushing them both and then straight back in the cot.

I texted my neighbours and told them I was sleep training and sorry for extra noise as I knew through the night was going to be tough. By the third night my boy twin didn't bother to even cry when I left and his sister probably took a week to stop crying the minute I put her down. Although I had a great bedtime routine, it probably took the twins a good few weeks to stop waking during the night but I continued to use the same method of controlled crying and each night got better and better.

Now they don't cry when I put them to bed and they sleep through the night for about twelve to thirteen hours. If they wake in the night they will usually settle themselves. Life is so much easier and the babies are very happy.

***

DEVELOPMENT

Moving

With the usual caveats of twins taking things more slowly at times, and not to worry too much if your two are developing more slowly than your chums' single-ton babies, it's likely that at least one of yours is crawl-ing or bum shuffling. The excitement and pride you feel when they really start to go for it can be quickly replaced by panic as you suddenly realise you're going to have two little ones going in different directions for some time to come. They may also start to pull them-selves up to standing and walk themselves along whilst holding on to furniture (known as 'cruising') and, yes, some will also be walking. You may worry about one twin's development being faster than the other, but be reassured that having them take their turns at these adventurous new skills at least lets you get your head around it – and better baby proof their surroundings.

Some mums will find playpens a godsend at this time, or might put a gate across the doorway of one 'safe' room, so they know they can pop to the loo without having to strap the babies in. Louise copied a twin mum friend and joined two playpens together, stashing all the toys in them. That way, the babies wanted to be in there and would choose to walk in and out of them. They would still cry when she closed them in and walked away, but, as soon as she was out of view, the babies would sit and play quite happily within a matter of seconds, and certainly long enough for her to have a quick shower.

It may also be time to start thinking about retiring/eBaying your bouncy chairs as the babies will soon be able to climb out of them. You certainly shouldn't leave them alone in bouncy chairs when not in the room with them. And remember, if you haven't already, to move the base of your cot down to the lowest level to prevent night-time escapes.

It's worth mentioning reins at this stage. They have much less 'dog harness'-looking ones these days, and many mums have found them useful, even those who had previously sworn them off. This includes Louise, who found them invaluable on London's busy shopping streets and in the shops themselves – cute designs (some have little backpacks) helped them and her feel better about it and old ladies were very understanding!

However, the twins will soon be moving in opposite directions when they are walking, so the reins can have limited usefulness.

It's still worth keeping them in the buggy and then possibly letting them take it in turns to walk alongside holding your hand or the buggy. That said, Louise's twins would scream blue murder to see their sibling being allowed to walk when they weren't, so this may not be plain sailing either.

***

Amber

Isla was crawling at seven months and the day she crawled was the same day she stood up – she was really mobile. I don't think Daisy crawled until eleven months; she used to roll everywhere to get things. She was really, really funny, and really, really fat! Isla was really agile and skinny and lean, and still is. Daisy walked at sixteen months, Isla walked at twelve or thirteen months. I've got videos of them and, now I watch them, I think they're really funny how Isla would move about and Daisy would just stretch and reach for things. I thought that was a really nice time – that's when we started getting out a bit more, going to lots of activities, because their necks were stronger and I could carry them more easily both at the same time.

Eleanor

One commando crawled and didn't really want to sit up for quite a long time. It happened one at a time, which helped. It does totally change things – before you could go and have a shower in the morning and you could put them in their chairs and know they would be there when you got back.

Elna

They were both bum shufflers, one after the other, but they were about fourteen, fifteen months before they started moving. They were even quite late sitting up. My son walked at twenty-three months and my daughter at twenty-four months, so really late. My arms looked like Madonna's.

Beatrice

Thomas is making progress. He saw a physiotherapist in the hospital because he had problems sitting on his own – now he can do it. Gregoire sat five months before his brother. Thomas is now kneeling up at twelve months. He is a little frustrated and jealous of his twin brother as he can do more stuff.

Lucia

They've been quite mobile and very free from the beginning – what I set out to do is leave them very free even when they were not walking or crawling. I had the whole room padded and baby proofed so if they wanted to crawl or just lie there the whole room was available. And I've opened the house to them little by little. They took their first steps at ten months.

***

Language

As well as crawling and walking, your babies will start to say words at this time. They may still only be intelligible to you and close family, but you will be able to discern what they mean, whether the first things they say are the dog's name or their version of 'milk'. If you've been baby signing you will also see it really take off at this time. It's not too late to start if you still want to, and does not hold back spoken language development.

Whether through the sounds they make or the signs they give you, they will be delighted when you recognise what they are saying. Around this time they may also say each other's names, particularly when parted for a short while, as they will likely find it very odd to be separated. Spending some time without their twin is a good thing from time to time if they are spending most of their time together.

It's also a good time to start thinking about teaching

them simple discipline words such as 'no', 'down' and 'gentle'. The fights over toys will start around this time, some hair pulling and pushing will more than likely occur, but hopefully you can minimise clashes by encouraging gentle touching and provide suitable distractions. A good rule to start with is to always give attention to the 'wronged' party (the twin whose toy was snatched or hair was pulled) so as not to 'reward' bad behaviour with too much attention, which they will fight for whichever way they can.

It's not necessary to buy identical toys, just things that are equally distracting – one could have a tambourine, another a shaker. If you have an older child or children you will start to see them playing together much more, but don't expect them to play very much as a threesome, more likely one twin and their older sibling. As people with three children will tell you, it's much more common that two will pair up leaving another to play (hopefully happily) on their own.

Play

Whether for practical or financial reasons, there may be times when you won't be able to get out too much and may find yourself at home looking for some fun things to do. These activities are not unique to twins, but work well with more than one baby at home.

DIY soft play – take your cushions off the sofa, pillows and duvet off the bed, and create a soft play area in your living room or bedroom. They will love climbing all over the different textures and heights, and delight in playing peekaboo with each other if you set up a few obstacles for them to peek around, or fabrics to lift up. Who needs parachute silks when you have an old duvet cover to float over the top of them?

Not-all-that-messy play – messy play can be frightening to a twin mum, thinking of double the mess to clear up as well as the floor after every meal. So, we would suggest setting up messy play in the bath, on the kitchen floor or in the garden. Get some water, strip them down to their nappies and give them some cups and spoons – they'll be happy for ages. If you have some strong closable plastic bags, you can also put different substances in them such as flour or shaving foam, and maybe some food colouring as well, and let them have a good squish (not a great idea for determined biters, though!). The large Aquadoodle mats that change colour with water are also brilliant for painting without any paint to clear up – they can use their hands or paintbrushes with plain water and the babies will feel like they are really painting. There are also some great recipes online for making your own playdough, which is much cheaper than the cartons in the shop.

Baby bandstand – put on the radio or a favourite CD and do nursery rhymes with actions, or just give them some musical instruments that you have or can make – wooden spoons and pan lids, empty water bottles or Tupperware with pasta or sugar inside. They'll have a ball and hopefully wear themselves out (which will make the racket worthwhile).

We hope you will have made some local friends with babies, whether twins or not, the same age as yours. 'Playdates' might seem ridiculous at this age but, again, a different set of toys, and taking it in turns to have your house turned over by the little creatures can make your day much more interesting, and give them the stimulation and activity they need.

DIFFICULTIES

Separation anxiety

This issue may raise its head just when you don't want it to. Just as you are feeling strong enough to leave them for a bit, and maybe thinking about going back to work, they start getting upset when you leave. Remember that, for the vast majority of them, the tears and upset will dissipate once you are out of sight (often in seconds). Get them used to you leaving the room and coming back, however painful it may seem – they need to learn that you say goodbye, they feel sad, then cheer up, then you come back and they're even happier.

As with all other developments you may find one is more affected than another. This doesn't mean you're doing anything wrong with one or not bonding enough – it's just another developmental stage that one may be ahead of the other on. *Owl Babies* by Martin Waddell is a beautiful book that might be good to read with them at this age. It is about three baby owls who find their mummy has gone away and worry for different reasons until she comes back and reassures them.

Competing for your attention

A good and simple piece of advice that was given to Louise before giving birth was 'get relaxed about crying'. Although your babies will be so much easier to please these days, there may be moments when both are crying and both want mummy (yes, sorry dads, it will still be mummy for a while), and it'll be very hard to attend to them both and not get stressed – especially as they can say 'mama' so clearly now, and can determinedly push each other out of the way.

Our best advice is sit on the floor and cuddle both as best you can. But if it's too hard, one will have to cry for a bit until you can swap over. From anecdotal evidence, however painful it is to parents, twins seem to become more self-soothing as a result of having to wait their turn. For example, once when Louise decided it was her boy twin who needed the first hug, her daughter stopped crying, made the baby sign for her older brother, Thomas, and crawled out of the room looking for him!

Getting sick

The more you take your babies out to explore their surroundings, the more likely they are to pick up bugs. Expect your twins to pass bugs amongst themselves – some even suggest trying to make them share bugs when you realise one is sick so you can deal with them both at once (especially if you're back to work). We think it's easier to deal with one sick baby at a time on the whole, however. If it's really difficult and you and they are both suffering, please retire to the sofa for cuddles and CBeebies. It won't be forever and it doesn't make you a bad parent.

Getting out and about

Whilst life is easier and the babies are very entertaining at this age you may, to be honest, find yourself itching for a bit of variety in your day. Getting out and about needs to be part of your week, and classes such as nursery rhyme singing sessions will be much more enjoyable for them now (even if it's still quite a physical and mental effort for you). They will start doing the actions to nursery rhymes soon, so keep it up and you will be delighted with their first visual renditions of 'Twinkle Twinkle' or 'Wind the Bobbin Up'. There are often free sessions at local libraries and, if you're lucky, the person holding the class may help you with a baby or the babies may even be happy to watch and listen from their buggy. Soft play centres often have baby areas as well, which are well worth spending a bit of money on if you can. It's really lovely to see how interactive your babies will be with other babies (plus you get to sit down on a crash mat and watch them for once, safe in the knowledge that they can't go anywhere or do any damage).

GOING BACK TO WORK

If you are going back to work, it may be full-time or part-time. This will depend on many factors, including the nature of your work, your financial situation and your childcare arrangements. Keeping in touch days – when you go back to work during your parental leave for meetings, trainings or just to see how things are working – can be very helpful for testing the waters and to see how it feels to leave your twins for a few hours or a day, and see what happens when you come home and what state the house and the babies are in. It is a slow transition and many twin parents have said this helped a lot. Every employee has the right to ten paid keeping in touch days but you don't have to take up the offer. We realise this isn't much help financially for freelance or self-employed parents, but the principle of doing some work during your parental leave (maybe attending a networking session or meeting with a long-standing client) is a good one.

Finances are a big consideration and this will ultimately be a decider in whether, how, when and where you return to work. It will also affect what childcare you choose. Many twin mums delay going back to work because childcare costs are too high and it is not worth it until their twins are getting some free childcare from the government. At the time of writing, some children are eligible for free childcare from when they are two, for example, if parents are in receipt of a qualifying benefit such as tax credit for low income or the child has a disability, which will increase after the school term when they turn three, when all children are entitled to fifteen hours of free childcare. Ask your health visitor about this or look up the latest entitlement at gov.uk.

It may be that you don't want to go back to work and want to be a stay-at-home parent. Sometimes we think we want to go back to work and realise we prefer to be at home or vice versa. There are no rights or wrongs, just what is right for you.

Ella found the decision to return to work very hard and took a career break before making a change in direction.

***

Ella

I felt like I was due to go back to work just as my girls became more fun and more interesting and the fog had lifted. I just was not ready. It is a tough decision and at times I did not feel I could talk to anyone about it, especially as I knew some mums who wanted to go back to work for their sanity and others who were prevented from going back to work because of the prohibitive cost of childcare. In the end I managed to get some careers counselling through the NHS (my employer at the time) which helped.

I sometimes felt that society frowned on me for taking time out of my career and being with my three children. There was a real pressure to go back to work and be a career woman. However, just as much as I felt a pressure to return to work, others who go back to work feel a real guilt about not being at home with their children. Sometimes it feels like you never get it right and you are never on top of work or home and are split in more than two ways. There really are no rights or wrongs, but I do not think I can have it all – a successful and ambitious and full-on career and to be there when each one of my three young children needs me.

What is also surprising is that they seem to need me more as they get older – not in the physical sense of feeding or changing but in the emotional sense of being there to listen and comfort.

Louise
For both financial and intellectual reasons, I knew I would be going back to work soon after the twins turned one. I had happily taken voluntary redundancy whilst pregnant with George and Alice so needed to find work and decided to be

a part-time digital consultant, working no more than four days a week. My other three full days at home, plus four days of bath and bedtimes, made me feel like I was still the one doing most of the parenting, and gave me enough time to pick up meaningful work where I could make a positive impact. However, my part-time options were much worse paid than the job I had left, which became disheartening. I was barely covering the cost of childcare, doing less–than–ideal jobs, and we were all missing each other. A year on from that, the work I am getting is much more interesting and better paid, and the less-than-ideal work actually proved incredibly useful, feeding into the more fulfilling work I'm picking up now. We all still miss each other at times, but I am also happy they get lots of stimulation from a great nanny, fun activities, one another and their older brother.

CHOOSING CHILDCARE

If you are going back to work, choosing childcare is a necessary and daunting task, especially for the first time. The following advice goes from the cheapest to the most expensive options, with advice for getting the best option for each.

Whatever kind of care you choose, it is vital that

your children form a strong bond with at least one person whom they can go to when they need help or comfort. Some mums find the idea of their child forming a strong bond with another person strange to deal with, but it is important that they feel loved and safe wherever they are and whomever they are with. It is also essential that you take up references or talk to other parents who have used a nursery or childminder – do not be shy about this, you can ask questions about areas you are unsure of, and get a much more rounded picture of individuals' and places' strengths and weaknesses.

MEMBERS OF YOUR FAMILY

If you have family that are willing to do some childcare or share it between different grandparents, for example, then you are saving a lot of money and it is lovely for them to have this bonding time. It is important, however, to ensure there are clear expectations and boundaries – parents often find grandparents are more lenient for example with screen time, unhealthy foods and bribes! If they are acting in the place of a parent for any significant stretch of time, you will need to discuss what your expectations are before you start the arrangement (and maybe come to some compromises over the biscuits but be firm about any consistency of parenting style that is most important to you). Don't assume it's OK to be late because it's a family member and, remember, looking after two can be very tiring for older members of the family. Consider discussing openly a trial period to check it's working for all of you (ideally away from the children – maybe a 'thank you' cup of tea at a café or dinner out), so you have some dedicated time and space to talk through how the arrangement is working.

CHILDMINDERS

Childminders usually work out one of the cheapest of the paid options. As with nurseries, good childminders may get 'booked up', however, so investigate as soon as you can. As with all caregiving, childcare providers can vary greatly – some childminders feel like a mini nursery, others are mums fitting your kids in with their own children which, with the right relationship and matching values, can be a lovely home from home. All childminders will need to be Ofsted registered, and have first-aid training and DBS checks as standard.

Registered childminders can look after up to six children up to the age of eight. Of these, a maximum of three can be under five years old, who are classed as 'young children', and a single childminder can only have one child under one year old although they can apply to Ofsted for an exception for twins (or they may have an assistant). This ratio includes the childminder's own children if they are under age eight.

Things to know about and questions to ask a childminder

Paperwork

Firstly, there are the basics that must be covered thoroughly – you want someone experienced, with training, maybe some relevant qualifications, with the necessary insurances in place. Their first-aid training must be no more than three years old, they should have food hygiene certificates, maybe a Certificate in Childminding Practice or NVQ 3, and have good contracts – including details on how holidays are agreed between you – ready for you to read through.

Experience

Don't get hung up on having experience of having looked after twins although that can be reassuring – looking after two children at once of very similar ages will be really valuable experience too.

Their care

Most importantly, after you've heard hopefully reassuring facts, how do you feel about their care? Visit whilst children are there, and always take up references. Do the children look happy, occupied and like they all have a good relationship with the childminder? Are they easily asking for help or support, for example? If any are upset or there are disagreements, did they handle the situation well (which may not always mean intervening)? What are the rules around cleaning in the house, for example shoes on or off and hand-washing. Ask open questions such as 'What are your house rules?', 'What would a typical day entail?' rather than leading them to answers. If there are children from more than one family within the home, ask how they cope with any differences in expectation of behaviour or differences in parenting styles. As with most interviews, your mind may be made up within minutes, but keep listening out for any doubts that creep in. You want to be sure this is the right place for your children.

The environment

Do insist on a good look around – all the rooms, bathrooms, kitchen and any outside play areas. If there is no outside play space, how will they make sure your children get the chance to play outside?

Logistics

Where will the children rest? How will you find time to talk about how the children are getting on?

Further feedback and ongoing questions

It's important to agree a time maybe once a week where you can spend a little longer at drop-off or pick-up time to have a more relaxed conversation about their progress and any issues that may have arisen. If there are other things you want to know, don't be afraid to ask. Good childminders expect you to ask questions and will be happy to answer them.

NANNIES

A nanny can be cheaper and more convenient than paying for two babies at nursery (nursery fees can be higher for babies than older children as they require more people to care for them), although we feel obliged to mention up front that a very experienced nanny can be more expensive than nurseries. If you have another child to drop off and pick up from school, or need to minimise any unexpected time off work (with twins meaning twice the risk of illness, you may need to send one to nursery and stay home with the other) then a nanny can be both cost-effective and convenient. Your nanny may well have twin experience, although this is rare – but it's definitely worth asking on local twin groups (online) for any recommendations from other mums. The most important thing about nannies is chemistry – you should get on well with them and share the same approach. They should have great references and experience of caring for more than one child, and experience with children at the same age as yours. The nanny should be able to take your babies out to various groups and playgrounds and help with their food preparation, tidying up after them and doing their washing (but not yours).

Nannies can be found through an agency which deals with the references, DBS and so on but has an agency fee, or by yourself through personal recommendations, or Gumtree, Mumsnet or websites such as childcare.co.uk (where you can also ask for part-time hours if you only need two or three days per week, e.g.). Given the age of your children, it's unlikely you'll find a nanny who will want to nanny share with new twins and another child from another family, but that may change as they get nearer school age. You need to look into this a few months before going back to work and have interviews with prospective nannies. Nannies are usually on a month's notice, so looking a couple of months before you need the care is probably the minimum time you will need. A good nanny will have some form of childcare qualifications as well as appropriate experience or possibly just tons of experience (that can be verified through watertight references) and will be happy to take part in a formal interview.

Create a shortlist of candidates that you are definitely sure are worth interviewing – aim for around three to five the first time you interview. You will be able to tell from their experience whether they are worth speaking to, and lots will supply written references with their CVs. It is acceptable to ask nannies back for a second interview before making your decision – always have one when the children are there so you can see how they interact with each other and consider another in the evening, if appropriate, maybe with your partner or a trusted family member.

Practically, you want a good cook (who can prepare fresh, healthy foods from scratch) and someone who will research the latest classes for you and make suggestions based on your priorities and their observation of what your children are enjoying or where they need to develop. Make sure that they are very comfortable with outdoor play (potentially in cold weather as well as warm), as gross motor skills are incredibly important when the twins are newly mobile.

Good chemistry with you, shared values and the ability to non-defensively take feedback and criticism are essential. But, most importantly, a loving pair of arms, patience for two (especially when both are crying) and a great sense of fun are most important when they are this little.

Examples of questions to ask a nanny

What do they love about your children's age? This will test their knowledge of child development, plus give you a nice feel for their style and interests.

When do they think the challenging times will be when caring for your children?

How will they manage two?

When have they disagreed with a parent over something for a child in their care?

How did they handle it?

What's the best relationship they've had with a parent or family?

What was so good about it? Some nannies basically want you to butt out and let them get on with it – which may work for you – but it may be more important that you find someone who has worked well alongside another parent.

First-aid competence

If your child has allergies or regular medication they may need, do they have experience of that? For any child, a good question around first aid might be, if they noticed some breathing difficulties, what would they check for? When would they call 111 or go to A&E? These scenarios aren't likely to happen but it's so important to know that their first-aid knowledge is comprehensive and up to date.

Above all, listen to the little voice in your head that says 'I like/don't like this person' but don't expect perfection – but then it's really important to push any of the references (have phone conversations with the previous employers) on any areas that you might have questions about. Do ask about sick leave records too – you really want someone who won't be taking extensive time off!

It's also very common to ask nannies to provide a daily diary of what the children have been up to if you would like this – what they've eaten, when their nappies were changed plus any new things they did or experienced – so you are aware of their day and don't feel like you're missing out.

NURSERIES

Many parents, however, prefer the idea of their twins being in a nursery so they can meet other children and get to do lots of activities (but beware extra charges for these!). Most nurseries assign at least one key worker to each child so they will still be forming strong, caring relationships with named individuals. You are much more likely to find one of the staff members who has experience of twins, and good to know that at least one of your children is assigned that person as you may prefer different key workers for each child. Some nursery fees cover the cost of nappies, food, classes and activities – but not all. Make sure you check for a full comparison with your other options.

Good nurseries can have very long waiting lists for places, so it may even be worth registering while you are pregnant and definitely worth visiting as early as you can. Unfortunately, some charge a non-refundable fee for registering your interest. Anecdotally, some parents thought that nurseries prioritised parents who wanted full-time places, with part-time places not being confirmed until very close to the time parents were going back to work – so you may also need to hedge your bets and put deposits on more than one nursery.

Some nurseries have a very homely feeling with lots of freedom for children to roam around, while others are more structured around educational activities (although this would be unusual for children as young as one). As with the childminders, you will get an excellent feel for a nursery when you visit – are the children well occupied with an interesting variety of activities that are allowing for lots of different types of play? How and where are babies and younger children cared for in comparison to older children? Do toys look well loved but clean? Would you be happy with your child crawling on their floor? What is their policy around lateness (which may be unavoidable in your work)? You may also find the quality of food varies greatly and this may be important to you – packed lunches are necessary at some nurseries, but others don't allow you to bring your own food. Remember that nurseries are businesses and can have good and bad managers – what is their staff turnover like? Can you speak to some staff members or are you just talking to a manager? Do staff members seem happy with their place of work and have nice areas for them to rest and relax in away from the children?

Nurseries can be wonderful but also rather busy, daunting places for babies that have been largely at home with you, so it's also good to ask about settling-in periods and how they handle any difficulties at that time. Speak to parents who have actually used the nursery, maybe even had the same key workers if possible. On those days that neither you nor the babies want to be parted, it will make that separation so much easier the more confident you feel about the arms you are leaving them in.

OTHER FORMS OF HELP

If you work from home or you just need some additional help as the babies grow older, the following may also be suitable for your circumstances.

MOTHER'S HELPS

A mother's help is often someone who comes for less than full-time hours, is unlikely to have the same child-care qualifications as a nanny and is not initially left in sole charge of the children (i.e. a parent will also be present in the house) but should have good experience with children. Mother's helps will have more general household duties such as cleaning, laundry, cooking and errands (but are not cleaners). Mother's helps can work really well for parents working from home, or part-time working or those with other children or caring responsibilities. With younger children under two, mother's helps can sometimes take sole charge but they would normally require supervision at first (some mother's helps may then develop enough experience to become nannies). Mother's helps can live in or live out and work as many hours as is agreed and are paid at a lower hourly rate than for a fully qualified, sole-charge nanny.

AU PAIRS

Au pairs are young people looking for a family experience and to improve their language skills in another country. They always live in and should be prepared to do light housework, babysitting and some cooking, but must be given time off for study. They may have some childcare qualifications but are usually not suitable to be left in sole charge of children under two. Maximum hours for au pairs are around thirty hours per week (including babysitting), but often those classified as 'au pairs plus' will work for up to thirty-five hours. This could work well if you need help with older children going to school but obviously you will have to have a spare room. In terms of hourly cost, au pairs are much cheaper but are not a childcare solution for those returning to work with preschool twins.

WHAT'S IT REALLY LIKE?

For most of us this really is a golden time with tons of smiles and laughs, loads of photo opportunities and just enough mobility to keep them happy and excited, but not so much to give you a massive headache. It should be more than possible to take the babies out (not so many milk feeds) as long as you're equipped with snacks, wipes, nappies and changes of clothes. You may be about to go back to work, so make the most of it. But don't worry too much about how many classes you go to for their development – they have you and each other for stimulation and cuddles and as they grow older they will get a lot more out of music and gymnastics!

Do celebrate their first birthday party for your own sake – make it a celebration of you all getting through this first year. They don't need an entertainer or even any friends there – but feel free to invite your own supporting cast of friends and family. And as for presents – they'll be happiest with the packaging anyway! Use this birthday as a moment to pat yourself on the back for a job well done, to say thank you to the people that have helped you through it and to celebrate the wonderful little lives that have just begun on their own exciting journeys.

We asked our panel of multiple mums what the best part of the first year was…

***

Amber

I really loved it, I really love being a mum, it's the first time I've ever felt like 'I'm good at this'. I didn't feel like I couldn't handle it. When you have twins it justifies that feeling even more so you feel 'I can do this!' We just felt we were really, really lucky having two – but maybe we wouldn't if we hadn't had so much trouble having the girls. I think, for me, because of that I did sit back and really enjoy them. I think sometimes you've just got to stop and watch them and I made sure I did that. On loads of occasions just sit back and watch them – we weren't doing anything, I wasn't in a rush to do anything, the only thing we had to do was buy some bread if we went outside, the experience was really enjoyable. They are still great. I love being with the girls, I didn't go back to work so I spend a lot of time with them.

Elna

I really genuinely loved all of it. It's obviously a lot of work, but I haven't needed help and I've got out every day on my own. For me, seeing them starting to interact with each other, and when they start smiling at each other and giggling, and seeing their eyes follow you round the room, and seeing that bond starting to come, was all really special.

Katie

I guess it feels like we're a big family, which is what we wanted.

Rachel

Having newborns when they sleep together and they curl up and there's that connection between them. Needing all that attention – for all that it can get a little bit annoying, it is a reminder of how special it is to have two at once. Which is a good thing to remember when you're absolutely exhausted and you've already changed twelve nappies and you haven't had time to have a shower… It is pretty magical.

Lucia

I was in awe whatever they would do. I don't think I've ever been as happy in my whole life; the whole experience has been unbelievable. The fact of having two babies and having them interact with each other – to see them grow from just being two babies who don't recognise each other, or know there is another baby next to them, to recognising the other baby as their brother.

Hugh (Ella's husband)

Having twins – it's incredible! You will experience things that other parents won't. It's wonderful watching them develop, seeing how they are so similar and yet also develop their own unique personalities. All the hard work is worth it a thousand times over. And once they get a bit older it is often easier having twins. They will go to the same school at the same time, want to see the same movies, do the same activities, have the same bedtimes and so on. So, they can be easier than having two children of different ages. And because they are always with their best friend and play so much together, they can be less demanding of your attention. But most of all it is the most amazing fun; I highly recommend it!

Afterword

As we finally finish the book, Ella's girls are about to turn nine, Louise's twins are seven and both our older boys are well established at junior school. We have had a good lesson in managing jobs, family life and writing a book at the same time – it's not easy!

We have tons of people to thank for their input and time in writing the book – a massive thank-you especially to Jo Feary and Alison Ive for so thoroughly reading the book and giving invaluable feedback and support. To Dr Ellie Cannon, Dr Sue Laurent, Dr Caroline Fertleman and Clare Byam-Cook for giving their expert feedback and support.

Practically we couldn't have done without Aiden for editing (before Unbound's editors stepped in for final polishing), Cary for the illustrations, Gilla for our video and our husbands and families for all their contributions and patience over many Monday nights and late-night Skype calls.

There is another page of thank-yous to all our financial supporters, but seriously – so many of you we know are not planning on having twins any time soon – it's so utterly lovely of you to support our book. We hope the generosity of your support will help others have a much smoother journey through their start to twin parenthood.

And an ENORMOUS thank-you to all the parents who answered surveys, were interviewed multiple times along the way and especially those who agreed to have their quotes featured in the book, namely Alison, Amber, Ann-Marie, Beatrice, Eleanor, Elna, Emily, Georgina, Jibecke, Jo, Judith, Katie, Lucia, Martina, Rachel, Sally, Sara, Vic – the experiences you told us about have shaped what we have written and represented; we hope you feel proud of your parenting looking back at that time and we are incredibly grateful for how generously you shared your stories.

We have learned a lot along the way and hope one day to share more perspectives on the next chapters of our lives as twin mums. We are still great twin mum buddies, still having conversations about our families' health and happiness, still trying our hardest not to compare or worry too much about their latest challenges. Above all, we always remember how fortunate we are to have our families and friends, so our final and biggest thank-yous are reserved for our husbands Hugh and Rob, our precious firstborns Joey and Thomas, and the four who started us on this journey – Leila and Miri and George and Alice.

Unbound is the world's first crowdfunding publisher, established in 2011.

We believe that wonderful things can happen when you clear a path for people who share a passion. That's why we've built a platform that brings together readers and authors to crowdfund books they believe in – and give fresh ideas that don't fit the traditional mould the chance they deserve.

This book is in your hands because readers made it possible. Everyone who pledged their support is listed at the front of the book and below. Join them by visiting unbound.com and supporting a book today.

Rachel Bellinger
Gemma Brady
Ally Branley
Susan Brown
Emily Carter
Avivit Caspi
Dr Choukeir
Rachel Craig
Simon Crook
Jonathan Davenport
Nicole Davis
Antonia De Feo
Nicklas de León Persson
Marisa Doberman
Naomi Edwards
Leonie Eisenberg
Ana Maria Florea
Naomi Goldstein
Sarah Goldstone
Clara Gonzalez
Caroline Greenberg
Sara Handman
Lee Hardman
Chris Harper
Martha Henson
Thomas, George
and Alice Hurd
Lily Ickowitz–Seidlet
Jill's Night Nanny Services Ltd
Dan Kieran
Hilary Knight
Jessica Kyriacou
Francesca Leigh
Maxine Levy
Carol Mackay
Chris Maiden

Julia May
David McGirr
Sam McGregor
John Mitchinson
Virginia Moffatt
Joane Monsanto
Jessica Muir
Mar Munoz
Emily Murray
Carlo Navato
Elizabeth Nortey
Joana Nunes
Sheena Peirse
Justin Pollard
Annabel Port
Ella Rachamim
Anna Rafferty
Vincent Raison
Laura Ramazzina
Cassie Robinson
Oliver Rosen
Francis Rowland
Laun Ruttenberg
Joan Ryder
Katie Schwartz
Aiden Selsick
Kate Shepherd
Georgie Shmuel
Jeff Stafford
Abigail Symons
Rosie Tasker
Vicky Taylor
Mark Vaughan
Tassie Weaver
Emma Witcoop
Su Zafar